Advance Praise for *Showtime!: The Greeting Card and Gift Company's Guide to*

"This book is the definitive bible for new and seasoned manufacturers in the greeting card and gift industries. It is one of the most important investments a business can make in preparation to exhibit at a major trade show. *Showtime!* is a book that is meant to be well loved. If your copy isn't dog-eared, highlighted, and bookmarked by the time you're done reading, you are doing something wrong!"
   —Carina Murray, principal, Crow and Canary

"Meryl Hooker and Rob Fortier are two of the champions of the greeting card industry! *Showtime!* should be the 'bible' for anyone planning on exhibiting at a trade show. This book will become the standard for trade show preparation and how to make the most of exhibiting your product."
   —Dorothy Creamer, editor-in-chief, Greetings etc. magazine

"If you're lucky enough to have found *Showtime!* before your first trade show, be smart enough to read it. It will not only save you time and money, it will spare you much of the anxiety that comes from inexperience."
   —Michael Caulder, Nuk-u-lur Greetings

"This book tells you upfront the reality of what's needed so you don't go in blind. For artists who are shy, it also gives a step-by-step guide for talking to a buyer to eliminate the extremes of freezing silent or overwhelming them with a sales pitch. Finally, a book that interviews real artists with real experiences, and not just professional trade show spokespeople."
   —Kate Harper, Kate Harper Designs

"This book is a crucial primer for those interested in exhibiting at trade shows in the stationery and gift markets. From setting achievable pre-show goals to following up on post-show leads, this book provides plenty of useful tips and advice that will not only save you money but your sanity too. Don't even think about doing your first trade show before reading it."

—Joyce Wan, Wanart

"This is not just a book about trade shows, but about customer information management, effective networking and all the tools a small business owner needs to be successful. Meryl and Rob get into the psychology of sales and the intricacies of business relationships in such a way that I found myself learning something new with the turn of every page."

—Stacey Rifkin, Hard Cards

"*Showtime!* should be read by all trade show newbies. It's filled with usable information detailing not only what to expect, but what's relevant to a new exhibitor. Overflowing with tips, helpful hints, and humor, it is a great resource and complement to *Pushing the Envelope*."

—Jennifer Nielsen, Wine Wear, Inc.

"Where was this book when I started exhibiting? Consider me jealous of everyone who is now able to read this great guide and avoid the pitfalls of the first time exhibitor."

—Amy Smyth, Amy Smyth Made It

"This savvy guide provides practical guidance and wisdom for those who are serious about growing a strong business. Rob and Meryl generously tell it like it is. This will be the go-to trade show resource for years to come."

—Geraldo Valerio, Urubbu Cards and Gifts

"Rob and Meryl have created a tremendous resource for card and gift industry producers who plan to exhibit at a wholesale trade show. I wish we'd had a copy of this wonderful tool before exhibiting our first time!"
    —*Sandy Dell, author,* **"The Complete Guide for Selling to Gift Shops"**

"There are so many things we have learned along the way that we could have learned just by reading this book."
    —*Lauren Gryniewski, Old Tom Foolery*

"After four years of exhibiting, I thought I knew all the tricks of the trade show. Boy was I wrong! Meryl and Rob have filled *Showtime!* with information I either never learned or I needed reminding of. Even a trade show veteran will wear out their highlighter on this book."
    —*Laurie Mee, Two Trick Pony*

"This fun, energizing read is an AWESOME, needed book that will help anyone who exhibits at a trade show. Even if you feel like you already know everything, this is a focused, consolidated view of how to be at the top of your game come show time."
    —*Scott Hay, Badge Bomb*

Also by Rob Fortier and Meryl Hooker

Pushing the Envelope: The Small Greeting Card Manufacturer's Guide to Working with Sales Reps

SHOWTIME!

The greeting card and gift company's guide to trade show success

Rob Fortier and **Meryl Hooker**

CENTER AISLE
PRESS

New York • Washington, DC

Published by Center Aisle Press. www.CenterAislePress.com

ISBN: 978-0-578-08158-8

To Stephen and Kyle

For always making us feel like stars

Acknowledgements

This book would not have been possible without the knowledge generously shared by so many people, both in and out of the greeting card and gift industry. We especially want to give a shout-out to the following: Terri Ann Brame, Lauren and Joel Gryniewski, Michael Caulder, Suzanne Karlson, Barbara Wade, Stephanie M. Fridge, Amy Smyth, Stacy Rifkin, Randi Picarelli, Greg Sargent, Megan Auman, Joyce Wan, Scott and Lauren Hay, Carina Murray, Carolyn Edlund, Dorothy Creamer, Kate Harper, Carrie Siegel, Laurie Mee, Craig Williamson, Geraldo Valerio, Jennifer and Jesse Nielsen, Sandy Dell, and our dear friend Jay Blumenfeld.

Rob: I would also like to thank Kenny Burrows, Mike O'Neill, and Michael "George" Rohrer for steppin' up when necessary.

Meryl: To the motley crew of manufacturers who have supported me in so many ways during the past 13 years, thank you. Super-sized love to Paul Boulais for his ideas and inspiration right from the zygotic stage of this project, as well as for being a damn good friend.

We especially want to thank Patti Stracher for her endless support, encouragement, patience, and humor with our irreverence, (okay, mostly Meryl's)—not to mention for writing such a kick-ass foreword. Our great appreciation and thanks to Stephanie Leon-Santiago and Natasha Davis of George Little Management as well.

Once again, we would not look nearly this good without the gracious editing assistance of Sally Murphy. Thanks for saving us from one more argument over commas and "stuff." And thank you for last-minute assistance from Simon Spelling. Your talents in the grammar and punctuation departments kept this project moving "foreword."

And last but not least, to Stephen Corsello and Kyle Todd, our partners in crime and in matters of the heart. There are just no words to express our appreciation and love for you. Thank you for everything.

Contents

Foreword

No matter how long we have been in our professions—no matter our niche, expertise, or industry connections—there is always more we can learn. This was surely my experience in reading Meryl and Rob's thorough and very entertaining second book, *Showtime! The Greeting Card and Gift Company's Guide to Trade Show Success*. I found myself nodding in agreement, pausing at an insight, and feeling downright satisfied at the end. This is the real deal on how to position your business for success when exhibiting at a tradeshow.

As Show Manager of the National Stationery Show, I have coached the full range of entrepreneurs over the years. I have worked with young owners of greeting card "start-ups" who have never been in business before, as well designers bringing considerable business experience to pursue their passion later in life. Many share a common element: they have never exhibited in a tradeshow and they do not know where to start.

Exhibiting takes a lot of planning and work. It also takes a willingness to learn a new language and skill set that might take you out of your comfort zone. Meryl and Rob very generously and very accurately lay this out for you—in the right order. This book contains virtually everything you need to know to get it right the first time: from planning and preparation, to designing your exhibit space, what materials to have on hand, show logistics, hotel and travel, the types of people you will encounter and even how to follow up when the show is over. Not to mention the supremely important (and often overlooked) subject of how to take care of YOU, before, during and after the Show. It is all here.

Even with all the technological tools out there, face-to-face business building will never be out of fashion. Tradeshows provide an excellent and very unique format for conducting business, networking, and socializing with others in our industry. This book provides an invaluable chance to learn important aspects of exhibiting before costly mistakes are made. It will help put your business on the right path to success. If you are a new exhibitor, there is much to learn these first few years and reading this book is an excellent first step in the process.

I am thrilled to have *Showtime!* available as a resource for our industry. I applaud Meryl and Rob for writing this book, and each of you for venturing into this great business.

To your success!

Patti Stracher
Show Manager
National Stationery Show
White Plains, NY
March 2011

Introduction

So, you're ready to exhibit at a trade show. Congratulations!

You've got the dream. You've got the vision. All signs are pointing toward exhibiting as the next step for your company. You are eager to get out on that big trade show stage where the audience will rise to its feet and throw money at you. You are anxious to make sales and promote your line. We get it. We've been there... a couple of times.

We aren't going to lie. At the most basic level, trade shows are ridiculous: spend thousands of dollars renting a space about the size of your bathroom for five days, stand inside it for 10 hours a day with your products on display, and try to make sales as potential customers walk past, often without even pausing to look at you. No guarantees. No refunds. Seriously, who in their right mind would do this?

Then, toss in the fact that exhibiting can be a huge financial gamble. Trade shows can push you to the edge and nearly break you. Plus, they require massive amounts of physical and mental stamina. Exhibiting demands deeper organizational skills and more patience than you ever thought you had. You must be nuts to do this voluntarily!

We agree. You have to be a little bit crazy to exhibit at a trade show. Welcome to the club! We've been waiting for you. But don't worry... you are in very good company.

When *Pushing the Envelope* came out in May 2010, we were bombarded with questions about the chapter on trade shows. Soon, we started getting requests to write a book about exhibiting. We were thrilled to answer the call.

As we began the process of talking to a variety of manufacturers and show producers about their experiences, we were amazed at the similarities in the stories we heard. It did not take long before we realized that as complicated as trade shows may seem to be, they actually all boil down to a handful of tasks and deadlines and a whole lot of hard work. More importantly, everyone is basically doing the same set of tasks and having the same frustrations. As you start down the road to a trade show—be it your first or your fifth—we hope you can learn from the experiences of others in the industry, or at least have a good laugh with them.

You know that exhibiting at a trade show is an important step to launching, branding and promoting your product. You have decided that now is the time, but where do you start? You probably have some specific questions. How should you budget for this? What do you say to people who come into your booth? How do you keep yourself in fightin' shape during the show? What happens after you get home again? How do you keep the momentum from the show going and your sales mojo flying high so you increase your likelihood of recouping you finances? For a handful of tasks, there is a lot to take in and consider!

Throughout this book, we have made every effort to include the most important aspects of trade show exhibiting. We hope you take the experiences we have shared, both good and bad, and use them to make the most of your trade show experience. We cannot promise that you will not make any mistakes, but we have given you the tools to avoid some of the major pitfalls.

Exhibiting at a trade show is making an investment in the future of your company; just like investing in the stock market, the payoff does not always come right away. Typically, when you buy stocks, you do not turn around and sell them the next day. You do your research; you watch the market; you make your move when the time is right and then hold onto those newly purchased shares. They may go up in value and they may go down, but over time it stands to reason that you will make money.

The same is true with investing in a trade show. You cannot just hand over the booth fee, show up with your exhibit and expect to double your money. You do your research first. We highly recommend attending a show before you exhibit to get a sense of what to expect. Take the time to make sure your products are ready to show. Your company will need to be prepared with a solid infrastructure, a business plan, and sales materials. Then you can make a commitment and prepare to exhibit.

What you get from a trade show may not necessarily be measured in financial terms either. There are many lessons to be learned when you stand in a 10-by-10-foot booth for four 10-hour days and some of them just might surprise you.

For the purposes of this book, we are going to make some assumptions about you and your company. Although we will touch on some basics, we assume that your product line is sufficiently developed, and that you have done your research and found a trade show that is appropriate for your products. We also assume that if you need help designing a trade show booth, you will seek it out. We make some suggestions, but will not be giving you step-by-step directions in booth design.

We assume you have (or will soon have) a signed contract, and have paid your exhibitor fee and received your booth assignment. Now what? That's where we come in!

So pack your bags and get ready!

You're going to Hollywood... or New York... or Atlanta... or Seattle... or Chicago... or, well, you get it. You're going wherever your business takes you.

Curtain up! It's *Showtime!*

**PART
ONE**

Pre-Show Planning

CHAPTER

1 Knowledge Is Power

Standing in your booth, writing orders and getting new customers is not the final destination on the road to trade show success: it is only the midpoint. The process of exhibiting is like the shape of a bell curve—a quiet beginning (pre-show planning), the wind-up and escalation to the middle (the actual time at the trade show), and the gradual retreat to the end (post-show follow-up). The most successful exhibitors have a plan that encompasses all three aspects with actions and strategies that are executed before, during and after the show. Sounds great, right?

The process of creating and implementing such a comprehensive approach may seem daunting to you. Please do not let it overwhelm you. You are probably already incorporating many of the components of successful show participation in your business every day. Framing these tasks in terms of a trade show timeline is just a more formal way of planning and strategizing ways to grow your business. By taking time in the early stages of your show preparation to construct a results-oriented action plan that includes a timeline, goals and even room for a little R&R, you will be well on your way to trade show success.

This section will walk you through the pre-show planning process. We will look at ways to get organized as well as help you create a plan to cover all your bases and return home again positioned to keep your show momentum going strong.

If you have ever worked with us before, you know we are big fans of lists and charts and planning. We understand that this approach may not be the most effective method for everyone. For the more creative types, this type of planning may seem completely restrictive and nearly impossible. You do not have to use our exact system, and we wholeheartedly encourage you to find a method that achieves the same outcomes in a way that works for you.

You certainly do not have to follow all—or any—of these planning ideas. But please understand: the strategies outlined here come directly from our combined 20 years of trade show experience as well as dozens of greeting card and gift companies we interviewed for this book. Please learn from our mistakes! Make your first time out a little easier—or at least more manageable—in whatever way that needs to happen for you.

To get started, let's look at the key areas to focus on before you even get to the show floor.

The Exhibitor Guide

Once you commit to exhibiting, you may be tempted to jump right into the deep end. A booth! You need a booth! Order forms! How many? Display features! Who will feed the dog while you are away? Book a flight! Do you buy an iPad? Get a hotel room! Where should you stay? What about shipping? Lighting? Do you need a haircut?

Stop!

You are getting ahead of yourself.

Before anything else, take some time to read the exhibitor guide. The exhibitor guide is the handbook of all the rules and regulations specific to the venue and the show in which you will be exhibiting. It is generally published by the show presenter or management company and is provided to you free of charge when you sign your show contract. This guide is an important tool for the adventure on which you are about to embark.

Inside the exhibitor guide, you will find details about almost anything you could want to know about the physical aspects of the show—such as booth logistics, freight information, official show publicity opportunities and show-sponsored events. You will also find guidelines for the types of materials you can and cannot use for your booth. Read these carefully and pay special attention to the details; it would be horrible to have to entirely reconstruct your booth the night before the show because your curtains and carpeting did not meet the flame retardant requirements.

Do not let the size of the guide overwhelm you. Not every piece of information in it will pertain to you or your booth. For instance, there may be an entire section detailing the rules and regulations for plumbing and water access for exhibitors. We have yet to see a card manufacturer that needed plumbing. But remember, the exhibitor guide is meant to be comprehensive; so even though you might not need to know plumbing rules, there may be a food company that does. (Though having a fountain in your booth would be really cool.)

"I was so frightened by the exhibitor's manual because there is so much in there!"—*Suzanne Karlson, Lumia Designs*

Give the entire exhibitor guide a quick read to get familiar with what is in there. You can skip sections that are not relevant to you on the second read-through. Take notes of anything you have questions about. Memorization of the guide is not required. There is no quiz at the end so do not let this become stressful for you. The point is to get familiar with the show rules, regulations and important deadlines. Even though there are hard deadlines and some potentially intimidating language, the exhibitor guide is actually in place to make your show easier. Please do not get overly concerned about the hard-and-fast rules. Exhibiting is exciting! Get ready to work hard but also to have fun!

Paying attention to the exhibitor deadlines is critical. There will be a deadline for everything from shipping and setup schedules to placing electrical and lighting requests. There will even be a cutoff date for ordering a trashcan. Be sure to pay special attention to these deadlines, because the last thing you want is for one missed detail to end up costing hundreds of extra dollars in freight charges or a lot of panicked, last minute rushing around.

Get Organized

Once you are familiar with the show guidelines, it is time to focus on getting yourself organized. Now is the time to revisit your earlier straight-into-the-deep-end freak out. We'll wait.

Ready? Go!

Feel better? Good.

Now, let's take all those ideas and questions and put them into a useable format.

Start by making a list of everything you need to do to get ready for the show—and we mean everything. The list may include booking flights and making hotel arrangements. It could also include researching, designing and ordering booth materials. Does your catalog need updating or reprinting? How about your order forms? Are you going to get that iPad? Are you going to have a giveaway in your booth? What type of pre-show publicity do you want to roll out? Do you need to update (or create) your website, or finally set up a Facebook or Twitter account for your business?

You may not even be aware of all you need to do or where to start, and that is okay. For now, just sit down and create a master list of things to do. This is a big brain dump of everything that comes to mind, including seemingly random things like buying new clothes, arranging for a pet sitter or even getting that haircut. It does not have to be perfect (and it won't be), or even necessarily complete at this point. Getting anything and everything down on paper will, believe it or not, help alleviate anxiety. It will also help you focus and organize your plan of attack.

Once you have your list, you may start to see how various tasks work together and even feed off each other. Sort your tasks into general categories so you can start to organize a production schedule. Here's an example of what this might look like:

Advertising & Promotions	Sales Materials	Personal
Design postcards to send to customers	Update and reprint a catalog	Schedule a pet sitter
Send out press releases about new designs.	Design takeaway postcards	Get a haircut
Set up a social media account	Pick out an in-booth giveaway	Break in new shoes

Create a Production Schedule

Now, take your big list of tasks and create a production schedule. A production schedule is a comprehensive list of all the tasks that need to be completed, and precisely when they are going to happen.

Create your schedule in whatever format makes sense and is the most workable for you. This may be on your computer calendar, a write-on/write-off wall or desk calendar, or even a paper planner. It can be a list in a simple Word document. The format is not important; what matters is that you create a schedule of deadlines to keep you on track as you count down to show time.

Start by marking the opening day of the show and work backward to today. Then, fill in any deadlines the show management has established in the exhibitor guide. These may include deadlines to place orders for show services, set up days, freight delivery days and important information about breakdown at the end of the show. Put down any show publicity and press deadlines of publications you want to send a press release to. Go through everything you have to do and assign it a due date. If you are updating and reprinting your catalog, when do you need to have the files sent to your printer? How long is the turnaround? Count back and figure out your deadlines and write them down.

Do this step-by-step breakdown for each item on your show preparation list. Some items will be easier to plan for than others. Your travel dates, or scheduling a reminder to change your outgoing voicemail message saying you are away at the Intergalactic Pet Paradise Show in booth 5555, will take less time than, say, designing your entire booth. It may seem silly to even put the easy tasks on the production schedule; nonetheless, go ahead and plan out those things now. As you get closer to the show dates, especially if you are shipping your booth to the venue, having simple tasks and activities already scheduled and planned will make life much easier and give you one less thing to think about.

Consider your arrival and departure dates in the show city. We definitely encourage you to arrive as early as possible and allow for plenty of time to set up your booth. After the show, you may consider hanging around for a day or so to visit with friends or family or just enjoy the host city. Regardless of what you decide, or can work out, put those dates on your schedule as well.

Look ahead to what happens after you return home from the show. Some of the most important—and profitable—work of exhibiting happens after the show is over. You are going to be tired and worn out after you get home, and not inclined to strategize anything more than a nap at that point. Take the time now, before the show, to plan out your post-show debriefing and follow-up strategy. This will keep you on track and help keep your show momentum going. Remember, the actual exhibiting part is only the midpoint of the trade show process. There is a lot that happens on the front and back ends that can help determine how successful your show will be.

We will go into much more detail about post-show strategies in Part 3, but start by listing out all the tasks you will need to accomplish once you get back home. These could include sending thank you notes, catalog mailings, order fulfillment, and invoicing. In addition to catching up on administrative work, be sure to allocate time for entering business cards into your database and for follow-up phone calls to prospective accounts, sales reps and retailers. You will want to include a general debriefing of what went well, and what you will do differently for the next show—because this time next year, you will not remember all of the important details.

Think through your post-show plans. What are you going to do to touch base with the customers and leads you meet at the show? If you are going to send out a post-show mailing, design and order those materials now so they are on hand and ready to go. For any email blasts you want to send out, schedule time to put together a graphics-based email campaign in advance. That way, all you need to do when you get home is load in the addresses, add a photo or two and hit send. Consider preparing any post-show website updates in advance as well, in order to make publishing them after the show a snap.

It is easy to get so lost in the planning that you feel like you are not actually accomplishing anything. The point of this production schedule is not to overwhelm you; it is to make sure nothing critical falls through the cracks. Take all the necessary little steps along the way to prevent being crushed and rushed. That last minute sense of panic will result in mistakes, missed deadlines and crazy decisions, like shipping your entire booth cross-country via 2nd Day Air (or something equally as nutty).

Set Achievable Goals

All this planning and plotting and scheduling is well and good, but how will you know if your trade show experience is a success? In a perfect world, we would be able to measure success just by the numbers: you hit it or you don't. Unfortunately, numbers do not always tell the full story of whether or not exhibiting paid off for your company. So, it is important to set some goals around what you would like to accomplish by exhibiting.

You might be thinking, "I've got some goals all right; I want to sell more stuff!" Of course you do, and this is an excellent start to setting a goal. But framed in this way, this goal is not measurable. There is no way for you to know when you have reached "more."

Goals need to be measurable in order for you to know you have reached them. There needs to be some kind of benchmark. If you were trying to lose weight, for instance, the first goal might be ten pounds. At least once a week, you would step on the scale and track the progress. If you never checked your weight, how would you know when you met your ten-pound goal? You could base it on how your clothes fit or if others are commenting about how extra-foxy you are looking. But without something solid to check your progress against, it is all guesswork. Your trade show success is no different: It needs to be measured by something more concrete than compliments.

What are some measureable and achievable goals you can set for your company at a trade show? Going back to the "sell more stuff" example, start by determining how much more you want to sell. Is it $500? $1,000? Whatever it is, write it down.

Some other achievable and measurable goals might be:

- Open 15 new accounts
- Meet 10 new sales reps
- Sign on 5 new sales reps
- Have 30 hot leads to follow up with after the show
- Meet 10 company owners with whom to network and find support

---

"We always say we'd like to double the past year, but that's not going to keep happening forever."
—*Lauren Gryniewski, Old Tom Foolery*

We all love to dream big, but it is important to be realistic. If this is your first trade show, it is not likely that you will walk out with 40 new sales reps and 200 new accounts. Yes, it could happen—and we hope you prove us wrong—but if you are not currently working with any sales reps, a goal of meeting and signing on five new reps would be more achievable. The point is to set show goals that will grow your company and keep you motivated, not to set you up to feel as if you failed.

Make Decisions

It does not matter if you have been in business 10 years or 10 minutes: there are some decisions that will need to be made as part of your pre-show planning. Many of these may already be incorporated into your daily business, but they are worth noting—especially if this is your first time exhibiting.

Credit Terms. Decide in advance how to handle credit terms for show orders. Will you require a credit card or prepayment for all new customers? Are you willing to extend terms to well-established retailers, even if they are new customers for you? There is no right or wrong answer to the credit terms question, but you will want to decide on a policy before you get to the show.

There will be some buyers who just assume, and expect to be granted, terms on opening orders. They will hand you a credit sheet and ask for Net 30 or even Net 60 terms right out of the gate. Until recently, it was not uncommon to extend terms to new accounts, provided their references generally checked out or at least looked good. The economic events of 2008 changed that business practice. Now, even large manufacturers require pre-payment on opening orders for new accounts, with few exceptions. If a store insists on terms, orders are generally held until a full credit check can be run. Again, there is no right or wrong answer. Just be aware that even the best stores can be slow to pay.

Also, be prepared for the fact that some buyers will ask you to call after the show for a credit card number. This is often the case on orders with future ship dates. If you agree to do this, know that it is not unusual to play a long game of phone tag trying to lock in those digits.

Minimum Orders. For the most part, the standard minimum order for greeting cards and gifts is between $100 and $150, whether a customer is ordering at a show or not. Decide what your minimum order requirement is going to be in advance, but be willing to be flexible on the show floor.

Show Specials. It is customary for exhibitors to offer some sort of show special. A show special is a promotion offered as an incentive to place an order at the trade show. Typically, a show special is free freight on orders over a certain dollar amount (usually $200 to $500, depending how your line is priced) or extended terms (such as Net 45 or even Net 60) to qualifying customers. Not all exhibitors offer a show special, but it can serve as the extra incentive an indecisive buyer needs to write an order.

You can make this really fun, too. Maybe your incentive is a "Pick Your Own Prize" Wheel where each square has a different discount percentage, free freight, free product or extended terms. When a store orders, they get to spin the wheel to find out which show special they have won.

"I offered 'No Minimum' as a show special, and not one person ordered below my minimum anyway."
  —Suzanne Karlson, Lumia Designs

Some exhibitors will hang a sign in their booth promoting the special. Others will just tell buyers if they ask. It is up to you how you want to handle it, but decide in advance. You do not want to be racing around at the last minute getting your signage together, or find yourself trying to track down half-inch dowel rods and a hot glue gun.

Exclusives. Some buyers will ask which stores in their area order your line. You may have an initial reaction of "That's none of your beeswax!" Sharing your customer list does seem a little counterintuitive. Why would you freely give that information away?

The answer is quite simple: retailers love to be the only store in a particular geographic area to whom a manufacturer sells its product line. This is known as having an exclusive. Some stores are very invested in having a unique inventory and will implement exclusivity themselves by not ordering if you sell to a competitor. Others don't care.

Will you grant exclusives? If so, how will you assign them? Manufacturers who grant exclusives typically do so by zip code; it is easy to track, and generally seems to be the most equitable way of dividing up retail territory.

Regardless of what you decide, it is a good idea to have easy access to your customer list at a show. If you are traveling with a laptop, have a copy of it on there. An alternative is to print out the list, sorted by zip code, and keep it in your booth. The method does not matter as long as you can access the information quickly. Of course, you may have all your accounts committed to memory and are able to recall every detail at the drop of a hat, but we somehow doubt that.

Staffing

"Never work a show alone." —*Amy Smyth, Amy Smyth Made It*

While it is certainly possible to work a booth by yourself, it is not the best way. We highly recommend you enlist the help of at least one other person to assist you for the run of the show—including setup and breakdown. Having another pair of hands will make your time on the floor much easier.

It also ensures you will always have someone in your booth, as well as someone who can help write orders and answer questions. When you get busy and have several customers in your booth at once, having help reduces the risk of losing sales with impatient or time-limited buyers who just move on. Even though you can always ask a show neighbor to keep an eye on things while you take breaks, being alone in your booth does not give you much of a chance to walk around the show. Walking the floor is an incredibly valuable aspect of exhibiting, and one that is easily missed if you are flying solo.

For the most part, it doesn't really matter who you have helping you; we've seen spouses, partners, moms, business partners, sales reps and even hired temporary help. Obviously, if you have staff at home, bring them to the show with you. Set up a schedule so that everyone has time for networking, meals and breaks. If you are working with sales reps, invite them to work your booth, too. It's a great way to get to know them and see them in action. You might even learn some new sales techniques.

No matter who you pick, just make sure to train them in the basics of your line before the show opens. It is important that your booth staff is fluent with minimum orders, shipping turnaround, best sellers, display programs and the show special. The last thing you want is an interested buyer asking a question only to be told, "I don't know. Can you come back later? The owner isn't here right now." A scenario like that sort of defeats the purpose of having help.

"Definitely have someone with you all the way from setup to breakdown, especially if your friend knows carpentry skills!"
—*Stacey Rifkin, Hard Cards*

Collecting Information

You will want to decide how you are going to collect information at the show. Many trade shows offer a scanner you can rent to collect information about visitors to your booth. Your smartphone may support an app that scans business cards as well. Some exhibitors just take a spiral notebook, staple business cards into it and take notes all in one place. Like other aspects of show planning, the methodology is not as important as having a plan in place.

Information gathering at a trade show may seem obvious, but a good friend of ours observed one of his neighbors throwing business cards into the trash. This neighbor admitted that she did not keep track of anyone who did not place an order at the show and that she did not maintain a customer database. We do not recommend this, especially if you are a young or first-time exhibitor. Following up with trade show leads is a key way to grow your customer base and your company.

Get a Customer Database

What are you going to do with all the information you collect? If you do not already have a customer database, getting one set up and ready to roll before you exhibit at a trade show is an excellent idea. There are many types of Customer Relationship Management (CRM) software programs available. As a new or young company, you may think you can get by using just a spreadsheet. Please do not do this. Invest the money into a real database that will capture, organize and allow you to manipulate your data. Setting this up from the beginning will save you hours of work down the road.

There are some fantastic and very affordable software programs out there that are easy to use, and many will even sync with your smartphone. If you are not sure where to start, just google "customer relationship management software" and do some research on which program is right for you based on your operating system and other technical needs.

At the very least, your database should include the store name, buyer name, phone, fax, email, website, order history (which products were purchased), and the dates orders were placed and shipped.

When taking on new sales reps, you will need to provide them with a customer list for their territory as well as any show leads. Having a database set up will make that much easier. Collecting and keeping this information updated as you go will also make catalog mailings and email announcements much more manageable. Your database will be an important way to keep track of leads and prospects from the show, too.

Your Unique Selling Position

Before you hit the show floor, you need to develop your USP, which is your Unique Selling Position or your Unique Selling Proposition. It is what sets your product apart from the competition and gives people a reason to buy from you. Your USP is an important part of product development and sales in general. It defines your mission, your purpose and your identity as a manufacturer. While it is not quite a magical love potion that makes customers fall for you, it is pretty close. A USP will also help you talk about your line to prospective buyers and sales reps on the show floor.

You should be able to get your USP down to one or two sentences. It is similar to having a business mission statement; the difference is a USP is targeted toward the actual product as opposed to what actions you are going to engage in for your business.

If you are feeling stuck on this, take a look around at other card and gift companies or even at other products you may already be purchasing. Try to identify the USPs of those companies and see how they are using them to develop their brand. Start with major, nationally distributed products since their USPs are easy to identify. Then, look at some smaller companies that you will not find in a big box store. How does your USP compare? Is it easy to identify? Is it easy to remember?

Here are some examples:

"Unsappy, uncrappy greetings and more." (Old Tom Foolery)

"Irreverent, snarky, eco-friendly greeting cards." (Hard Cards)

One way or another, you are going to need a USP; otherwise, you are just another card/trinket/gadget competing for a buyer's attention. Your USP may evolve as your line develops. In fact, it may completely change at some point. The important thing is to have a clear sense of what your product is and your specific target audience—especially going into a trade show. If you need more help figuring out your USP, please see our detailed discussion in *Pushing the Envelope: The Greeting Card Manufacturer's Guide to Working with Sales Reps* (Center Aisle Press, 2010).

By this point, you have already put in a good deal of work. You may be looking at this list of planning steps and thinking it is a waste of time; you can keep up just fine without it. You want to get to the fun stuff like designing your booth!

Trust us when we say it is not advisable or cost-effective to jump ahead without a well thought out plan. Getting ready for a show can be stressful and overwhelming, especially if you are a first-time exhibitor. You are going to be investing a lot of money in this venture, so please take the time to plan it out. Putting a plan together and having it in place well in advance will go a long way to keeping you (relatively) sane, not to mention on budget, during the months leading up to, and following, the show.

Every plan needs some financial backbone, and creating a trade show budget is critical to keeping you on track as you move toward opening day. So, dig out your calculators and get ready to think about money.

CHAPTER

2

Planning Your
Show Budget

"This thing can put you in the hole." —*Randi Picarelli, Hard Cards*

One of the biggest concerns you may have going into a trade show is the cost, and rightfully so. Trade shows are not inexpensive ventures. In fact, they may prove to be one of the biggest line items in your entire annual operating budget. No one likes unexpected expenses creeping up and derailing financial plans, especially profit projections. Planning a comprehensive budget can help eliminate some of the sticker shock of exhibiting. It will also give you a sense of what it is going to take to make money at the show or, at the very least, to break even.

So, what's the bottom line? How much is this whole thing going to cost? Unfortunately, there are no hard-and-fast numbers. For a regional show, the booth space may be a simple flat fee. Major shows determine the cost of booth space by square footage. At the risk of being completely unhelpful: you can plan on a trade show costing somewhere between $500 and $5000. There are simply too many variables to go into accurate specifics here.

For your initial estimate, your best bet is to contact the show you are interested in directly. Most shows have all of this information available on their website, or will have the contact information of someone who can help you with the specifics. Making an inquiry does not mean you are signing up for anything. Do not hesitate to contact show management with questions even if you are just in the consideration stage.

Planning a trade show budget can be challenging, especially for a first-time exhibitor; it can be difficult to know what it should include, let alone how much to allow for each line item. As with most things, it is best to begin at the beginning.

What to Include

Just as you did with the brain-dump To Do List, make a similar outline for your show budget. Here is a list of items to consider including:

1. Booth space cost
2. Booth design
    *   Hard walls, foam core walls, or curtains
    *   Furniture
    *   Carpet or flooring
    *   Signage
    *   Product samples
    *   Product display
    *   Electricity
    *   Lighting
    *   Audio/Visual equipment
3. Freight/delivery of materials to show
4. Drayage (moving your show materials from the loading dock to your booth)
5. Union labor, decorator fees, on-site show services
6. In-booth catering (for gatherings in your booth for sales reps or important clients)
7. Booth cleaning
8. Security (if you sell expensive or high-end items)
9. Insurance (shipping and booth contents)

10. Travel, including any checked or oversized baggage fees

11. Hotel

12. Food

13. On-site transportation (to and from the airport and convention center)

14. Giveaways

15. Office supplies for the booth

16. Product literature

    • Business cards
    • Other literature—sell sheets, postcards
    • Catalogs
    • Order forms

17. Staff

18. Advertising

    • Pre-show mailing
    • Post-show mailing
    • Advertisements in industry magazines
    • Show guide
    • On-site advertising opportunities

19. Miscellaneous expenses (there will be some—trust us!)

20. Post-show thank you notes and gifts

Even though this list might look excessive, it is important to include everything. It is much easier—and way more fun—to come in under budget than to add up your receipts after the show and discover you spent $150 on unplanned taxi fares.

"The first time I exhibited... I had the show labor forklift my pallet from the loading dock to the booth. At the shows I had exhibited at previously, this was included with the booth fees. The distance from the loading dock to my booth was probably not more than 300 feet. At the end of the show, I was slapped with a $500 fee and had to pay it as per the terms of my contract with the show. Lesson learned the hard way—always read the fine print!"
    —*Joyce Wan, Wanart*

Even though you will be looking to allocate dollars to a wide variety of line items, there are a few primary areas where the bulk of your show budget will go. These are: your booth, travel and hotel, sales materials, and advertising and promotional items.

Your Booth

Determining the cost of your booth space is relatively easy since that information is provided when you apply to exhibit. The cost of your booth structure, transporting it, and setting it up will probably be the largest single expense of your trade show participation; so much so that the price of the booth alone may be one of the determining factors of whether or not you exhibit at all.

For most exhibitors, designing the booth is one of the most stressful parts of exhibiting. How will you decorate it? Will you rent or buy furniture at home, on site or from the show management? What is the best way to feature your products on three walls?

You may already have ideas for your booth before you sign on the dotted line and reserve your space. If you already have a booth that you have used before, the planning process may not be a big a deal for you. But many of the exhibitors we talked to for this book reinvent their booth every year. Even with experience, starting with a blank slate can be overwhelming. There are many, many options available and this may be another point in the planning process where you feel like your brain is going to explode.

Much of what you need for your booth will depend on the type of trade show you are doing. Your vision for layout and design of the booth will also be a big determining factor in what you spend to outfit it. If you want your booth filled with LCD monitors with videos of dancing greeting cards, you are looking at a much higher price tag than using simple flame-retardant curtains and a rented table.

There are a couple of ways to keep your booth costs down, both in the short term and long term. Creating or purchasing a booth that will be used for more than one show will, after the initial outlay, help reduce your exhibition costs for future shows. Being able to reuse a booth, or at least parts of it, is definitely something to take into consideration, especially if you are investing a significant amount of money on display materials.

Another option is to rent or buy a booth package from a trade show company. Many of these companies will handle delivery of your booth to the show location too. Just be sure the booth size, contents, and shipping methods are in compliance with the show in which you are exhibiting.

"Don't feel like you need to buy every little thing that the trade show vendors try to sell you. You can put together a nice-looking booth without having to buy the plushest carpet pad or the fanciest booth furniture." —*Lauren Gryniewski, Old Tom Foolery*

Booth Setup Expenses

Depending on the size of your booth and the venue for the show, you may need to pay to have your booth assembled by someone else. Most convention centers have rules governing what exhibitors can and cannot assemble. Typically, exceptions are made for smaller booths. Show management contracts with a labor company to oversee the installation and dismantling (I&D) of the show. These tasks may be performed by union workers who will also be responsible for setting up the pipe and drape, show signage, and aisle carpeting. The labor company workforce also includes licensed electricians and carpenters.

If your booth requires electricity, hanging signs, or you need the use of a ladder or tools to install anything, chances are you will have to hire the I&D crew. You will be required to submit your booth plans in advance and get on their schedule. You should receive an estimate for these expenses so you will know in advance how much to include in your budget.

Please do not think you can break setup rules and get away with it. The I&D staff knows which booths they were paid to help assemble. You can be fined for doing unauthorized setup yourself, so play by the rules or be prepared to suffer the monetary consequences.

"I once installed my own lights at the Stationery Show. I stood on a chair and clipped them to the top of my booth walls. After the show, I received a bill for $50 from the Javits Center, which was for a half an hour of labor for the installation of my lights! Turns out I violated one of the show rules. I should have just hired the show's electrician to do it and saved myself the effort since I had to pay for it anyway." *—Rob Fortier, Paper Words*

Budgeting for your booth setup is more than just furniture and a pretty backdrop. Booth expenses can add up quickly so it is important to take the time to thoroughly research expenses and create a detailed show budget.

Travel and Accommodations

We are confident that, as a creative and resourceful business owner, you will find the most affordable means of transportation to the show. For budgeting purposes, book your transportation and hotel rooms as far in advance as possible. Discounts for hotel rooms are usually available through show management, so check the show's website for information. Please note: availability will drop as the show date approaches—especially for these discounted rooms. You know the show dates, so don't procrastinate!

"The plane tickets and hotels can be a huge chunk of change, so we start looking for deals pretty early."
   —Lauren Gryniewski, Old Tom Foolery

Do not be afraid to research lodging outside of the recommended hotels, too. There may be something that is comfortable and affordable that is not listed as part of the show's official hotel roster and is still in the area.

Give some thought to how close you want to be to the show venue. Remember, you will be spending eight to ten hours on your feet, and the idea of an hour or more commute to your hotel may be the thing that puts you over the edge. Yes, you may be able to save money on hotels that are further away, but by day three of the show, you will be putting great value on every minute of sleep you can get.

It is possible you will have friends or family in the cities where trade shows are held. As tempting as it may be to crash with them, our experience has shown that staying with friends often adds another layer of stress and obligation to a trade show.

One manufacturer we interviewed told us about how one of his reps asked to leave a trade show an entire day early to catch up on all the paperwork that had accumulated over the course of the week. When he asked her how this had happened, she said she was staying with her sister, who had booked dinner and entertainment every night while she was in town, and she was just too tired to process her orders.

Your days will start early and end late. By the end of the day, you may need some time alone. Plus, there may be additional paperwork to do in the evenings. Since none of this is conducive to being a houseguest, scheduling time before or after the show to stay and visit may be a better solution.

Sales Materials

Part of your show budget should include updating your sales materials. Many greeting card and gift companies update and reprint their catalogs in conjunction with a major trade show. If you decide to do this, be sure to include any graphic design and printing costs.

We encourage you to have some kind of update to your catalog available, even if it is a simple one-sheet with your new designs. This is a great way to get the attention of the buyers coming into your booth asking, "What's new?" or, even more directly, "Do you have a new catalog?" Your answer is then an enthusiastic, "Yes!"

A current, printed catalog is still an essential part of doing business in the greeting card and gift industry, and having a printed catalog available for distribution at a trade show is a must. Countless sales have been lost because an exhibitor did not have a catalog for a prospective customer and the customer was not interested in—or set up to have—a PDF version sent post-show.

"So many buyers walk the first day of the show collecting catalogs and come back and shop the subsequent days."
—*Stacey Rifkin, Hard Cards*

Catalogs do not have to be super slick and fancy but they do need to show your products with clear, high-resolution images, brief descriptions (if appropriate), style numbers and ordering information.

Having an organized, well-designed catalog that clearly shows your products is more important than having an expensive one. We have seen fantastic product catalogs printed on color laser printers at home. If you are exhibiting at a trade show, you probably already have a catalog; however, we would be remiss in our duties if we didn't reiterate their importance here.

If you do not currently have a catalog, want more information about catalog design or want a more in-depth look at the importance of having a printed catalog, please see the detailed discussion in our book, *Pushing the Envelope: The Small Greeting Card Manufacturer's Guide to Working with Sales Reps* (Center Aisle Press, 2010).

In addition to a catalog, you may consider having a general information postcard available as a takeaway in your booth. There may be some show attendees who do not want to take—or to whom you do not want to give—a catalog, and a postcard is an easy solution for this. Just like everything else, include any design and printing costs in your show budget. We will discuss takeaways in greater detail in Part 2.

Advertising and Giveaways

Naturally, many companies will increase their advertising efforts leading into a show. This can be an effective way to notify your customers you will be exhibiting, as well as generating traffic to your booth. As you put your budget together, consider some of the ways you can promote your company—both paid and free of charge.

Use Social Media. The least expensive way to promote your trade show participation is by using social media. Platforms such as Facebook, Twitter, and LinkedIn are a great way to let customers, sales reps and other industry people know you will be exhibiting and to give them your booth number.

Use these updates to talk about your preparation work for the show and give teasers about what you will be debuting. Talk about any show specials or promotions you may offer. We've even seen some manufacturers have a "Facebook Only" show special that was only announced on their Wall. If a customer came to the booth and said the secret word, they got a special deal.

You can streamline this process by using a service such as HootSuite.com to program your postings in advance. By investing a few hours, you can easily create a feed that runs for the next month and automatically updates your social media while you are getting ready to exhibit. Don't forget to include your booth number everywhere!

Mail to Your List. Send out postcards to your current customers as well as potential customers that you have in your database. Use one side of the card to feature your products and the other to announce that you will be at the show, your booth number, and that you will be debuting new products. Sweeten the deal by putting an offer on the card, such as free freight or 10 percent off if customers bring the postcard to your booth.

"I always do a [humorous] mailer to my current and potential customers with my booth number. When people come into the booth with the mailer, that's probably the most fun I have at the show." —*Amy Smyth, Amy Smyth Made It*

"We send emails to our best customers, letting them know about our booth number and reminding them to at least stop by and say hi, even if they aren't planning to place an order at the show."
—*Joel Gryniewski, Old Tom Foolery*

"One store said, 'We've been looking at your work for three years, and we got your postcard, and now we're finally ready to write an order.' This stuff works!"—*Megan Auman, megan auman*

Rent the Show List. Exhibitors often have the option to rent the buyer mailing list from the show management. The benefit of this is once you turn over your materials, your work is usually done. Typically, the mailing is handled directly by show management through an approved mailing house. Going this route also puts your promotion in front of every buyer who is registered for the show. The downside is the list rental can be expensive and you cannot target your specific market. Plus, the list cannot be copied for future use and you cannot mail the postcards yourself.

Sometimes a show will put together a postcard pack for several exhibitors. This may prove less expensive than renting the mailing list. The exhibitor guide will outline all these options. If you decide to go this route, carefully investigate and note the deadlines in your pre-show planning and budgeting process.

Buy Ad Space. Buying ad space is another way to promote your company. Ads are available in industry magazines as well as the show directory. The show directory is handed out to all attendees and contains a map of the show floor, a full show schedule and listings of all the exhibitors and their contact information.

Trade shows offer a myriad of other advertising opportunities, such as banners on the side of shuttle buses, lobby displays, and sponsorship opportunities. Many of these can be very expensive—and out of reach for most young and first-time exhibitors—but they are at least worth knowing about as you plan your advertising budget. Again, whatever you decide, be sure to include your booth number.

Giveaways

One of the fun things about trade shows is the cool giveaways. Everyone loves free stuff; and having something to pass out in your booth can be a relatively low-cost way to entice, engage and enroll new customers. Plus, it's pretty cool to see people walking around showing off your logo on a tote bag.

There are all kinds of giveaways you can offer. It can be as simple as a bowl with candy or as elaborate as a T-shirt. We've even seen exhibitors with show-specific items, such as magnets, notepads, pens and buttons, all with their company name, logo, website and show booth number on them.

"We've given away tote bags in the past and people seem pretty happy with them. Hard to say if it translates into higher sales, but it certainly doesn't hurt." —*Joel Gryniewski, Old Tom Foolery*

"One year, Old Tom Foolery gave out tote bags. Stacey and I spent the whole show being jealous. Those things were everywhere!"
—*Randi Picarelli, Hard Cards*

Freebies are certainly not required; and, if you are exhibiting on a tight budget, they are an easy line item to eliminate. The effectiveness of giveaways is also highly debated in different trade show circles.

"I do not think giveaways are that effective unless it's a giveaway of an item that you are actually also selling. I sell pinback buttons with my designs on them that I usually offer to prospective buyers at shows. It helps break the ice and has at times led to sales."
—*Joyce Wan, Wanart*

The easiest, and possibly #1, cost-effective giveaway suggestion we can make is a large bowl of individually wrapped mints. Trust us on this. You will be thanking us by noon on opening day. Three-hour stale coffee breath—that's all we're going to say about that. Most office supply stores or warehouse shopping clubs have industrial-sized bags of mints and hard candies for a minimal investment. You can even order them online.

If you are a candy or consumables company, have your own product available to sample—and be generous. For budgeting purposes, allocate an amount of product to put out for anyone who passes by your booth. Why reserve your samples for someone who has already agreed to place an order? They are already hooked! The purpose of samples is to get the attention of people who need or want your product but may not yet realize it.

Regardless of what kind of giveaway you choose, be mindful of the lead-time needed, especially if it involves custom printing. Include this cost in your budget; you do not want to be scrambling around at the last minute and paying lofty express-shipping charges to get your two-cent pens in time for opening day.

When creating giveaways for buyers, remember that unless it is consumable or useable on the spot, buyers will have to haul it around and get it back home again. Go for small, lightweight and easily transportable items, ideally show-related.

If you want—and your budget allows—go with something more elaborate. Instead of handing the buyer the gift, have a stack of mailing labels standing by;

simply fill out the label and offer to ship it home to them. This way, you only need to have a few samples of your giveaway on hand and not a full supply. With the mailing labels already filled out, mailing the thank you gifts will be a snap. Just be sure to include those shipping costs in your budget.

We will talk more about strategies for using giveaways to engage customers in Part 2, but for now just decide if you will have one, what it will be, and how much you are willing to spend on it.

"I used to have [chocolate] candy but people would stand in the booth and just eat it, so no more candy."
—*Amy Smyth, Amy Smyth Made It*

Booths and planes and money... oh my! Planning a trade show budget can start to take all the fun out of exhibiting. The good news is that once you know what your expenses are going to be, you can get on with the good parts of exhibiting—building your booth, setting up money-making strategies, booking company-growing appointments, and claiming your rightful place in the industry. But none of this happens if you don't have a booth. So first things first: let's talk about some booth basics.

3 Booth Basics

"Make the booth look like you want it to look but really keep expenses down. If something seems overly expensive, it probably is. Look into lower costs alternatives. Do some research."
—*Stacey Rifkin, Hard Cards*

It goes without saying that your booth design will be one of the main areas of focus as you get ready to exhibit. It can also be one of the most stressful. Your goal is to create an attractive environment featuring your products and giving a buyer a sense of what your company sells.

If you flipped directly to this chapter hoping to find all the answers about how to pick the perfect walls and where to get the cushiest floor pad, you may be disappointed. We are not going to explore the nitty-gritty, down-and-dirty details of building your booth here. There are hundreds of books and thousands of blogs already in existence that will give you complete and up-to-date information about the details of designing, building and sourcing your booth materials. If you need more information on the aspects of building a booth, we encourage you to check out those resources.

What we can—and will—do here is give you a general overview of things to consider as you integrate your booth into your overall show strategy.

As you put together your basic booth design, keep in mind that show attendees see hundreds of vendors and, after several hours of walking the show, many booths start to look the same. On average, you only have about three seconds to capture a buyer's attention, so make those three seconds count. This does not mean you should go over the top to make your booth stand out, but you will want to make sure it is memorable (in a good way).

The primary purpose of your booth is to feature your product. The second is to give a positive impression of your company. While a confetti cannon would certainly be memorable, it does nothing to promote your product—unless you sell confetti. Our guess is that most buyers would only remember your gimmick and walk away without any idea about what your company actually sells.

"Set yourself apart and really think about how to best represent your company. If you're funny, be funny. If you do custom stuff, people should know that by just walking by."
—*Randi Picarelli, Hard Cards*

Keep in mind that your booth is probably a small space, so sometimes less is more. Avoid the temptation to overload your booth with furniture and tables. Remember, your window to capture a buyer's attention is only three seconds. If they look into your booth and are overwhelmed by what they see or cannot figure out what you sell in the first place, they will just move on to the next booth.

"The first year I was panicked. I had way too much stuff in the booth. I had a table I didn't need. I had a fancy rug that was way too heavy to transport. I had too much trim and fancy stuff around my display boards. The key is simple: you want enough negative space so it doesn't look goopy. People are walking by in a rush, and they need to understand what is happening there."
- *Suzanne Karlson, Lumia Designs*

Designing your booth may be the most difficult part of exhibiting. You want it to look sharp, but you want it to be functional as well as portable.

Some Do's and Don'ts for Designing Your Booth

- **Do** make your signage clear and easy to read from a distance. You want someone to be able to read your sign from down the aisle.

- **Do** design your booth so that buyers can see and touch merchandise without having to enter your booth.

- **Don't** be afraid to strategically place items at the booth edge in order to capture a buyer's attention.

- **Do** make your booth easy to walk through. If a buyer needs to enter to look at products placed toward the rear, make sure they have an easy in and out.

- **Don't** set up your booth so buyers feel trapped when they enter. If they even suspect that there is a chance they will get cornered, they might just pass you by.

- **Do** practice putting your booth together at home. Hang up your backdrop. Set up and arrange the displays. Make a tape outline on the floor and arrange all the furniture inside the lines.

- **Do** make sure you have hidden storage space in your booth. This can be as simple as a draped table or a few baskets with lids.

- **Do** make sure your booth is well lit. Overhead lighting at a convention center is often insufficient on its own. Well-lit booths attract a buyer's attention; dark booths do not.

- **Do** make sure the booth is comfortable. Use carpeting or soft trade-show flooring. Your feet will thank you later.

- **Do** have room to do business. Even though you will be standing most of the time, have a place to sit with visiting buyers when it comes time to write orders.

- **Do** have fun with the booth. You want your booth to showcase your products as well as the personality of your company.

- **Don't** make your booth an obstacle course. Unless you have three or four booths to fill, go easy on the furniture.

- **Do** make sure your carpet or flooring lies flat. The last thing you want is a buyer tripping in your booth.

- **Don't** go crazy overspending on your booth. You spent time developing a budget so stick to it. Good booth design does not have to be expensive.

- **Do** spend the money necessary to communicate your brand with attractive and cohesive product displays and signage.
- **Don't** think you can break show rules regarding setup and get away with it. If the exhibitor guide says you cannot hang your own lights, then do not hang your own lights. Read about Rob's experience with this on page 22.

Getting Your Booth to the Show

For the purposes of this book, we are going to assume that you are not filling a 20-by-40-foot booth or having your own fleet of semi trucks delivering your materials to the show venue. We will assume that your booth will fit into a few boxes or shipping crates.

"When that box goes out two weeks before hand, you feel like you're getting your kid ready for Miss Teen USA. You know you can get things on the ground, but still, you want to be prepared going in." —*Randi Picarelli, Hard Cards*

To Ship... Or Not to Ship

If you live near the city in which the trade show takes place, you will probably be able to drive your booth and materials there and unload them yourself. If not, arrangements will need to be made to have your materials delivered to the show. There are a couple of primary options, but consult the exhibitor guide for specific information and guidelines.

Freight Carrier. When you use a freight carrier to ship your exhibitor materials, the company comes directly to your house or business, picks up your shipment and delivers it to the show on your target delivery date. A target delivery date is the earliest date and time your freight is allowed on the show floor; it is assigned to you by show management. After the show, the freight carrier picks up your containers at your booth and delivers them back to your home or, in some cases, on to your next trade-show destination.

Freight carriers have specific rules about how boxes are to be packed and labeled, so be sure to read all their guidelines carefully. It is essential that you adhere to the carrier's rules and the show's shipping deadlines.

"I had [lots of shipping problems] using a commercial delivery service. This year, I am going to have it shipped by freight."
—*Barbara Wade, Indigo Paper Goods*

FedEx or UPS. If you use UPS or FedEx, have your materials shipped to the show's warehouse. You will also need to make arrangements for delivery from the warehouse to the show floor. If you choose this option, be aware that you may incur a warehouse fee for holding your materials. You can also have your materials shipped directly to the venue according to the targeted freight deadline. Although you will not incur a warehouse fee, you may still be charged additional fees by the convention center.

Even though it may be allowed, we do not recommend having your boxes delivered directly to the convention center. Quite frankly, this is a terrible idea. The show venue receives hundreds of packages a day and you do not want your booth materials getting lost in the shuffle.

"Our first setup was super stressful. Our FedEx package with our catalogs and signs didn't arrive on time. So, the night before the show started we were at FedEx reprinting all of our signage and catalogs. It's worth it to ship your stuff freight rather than to try to pack it all into your luggage or send it in small batches via FedEx or something." —*Joel Gryniewski, Old Tom Foolery*

Hand Carry. Hand carry is just what it sounds like: you bring your own materials to the show and unload them. If you hand carry your materials into the convention center, you will still need to adhere to the targeted freight date. Do not think that you can set up early just because your booth fits inside a backpack.

It may be tempting to buy everything where you live, practice putting your booth together in your garage and then crate and ship the whole thing to the show. For convenience and efficiency, this may be the way to go; for exhibitors on a budget or those just looking to allocate their resources elsewhere, there are alternative ways of getting booth materials to their destination.

One approach is to ship less and then rent and buy what you need for the show on site. IKEA and discount department stores are great sources for inexpensive furniture and props that are easy to transport and put together. That table you really like may only cost $50 to purchase but you could rack up an additional $300 in freight to get it to the show. Before you buy, think through the most cost-effective options.

Besides having an official freight company, most shows have an official decorating company they work with. You can get everything from racks to carpeting to lighting to tables. It might cost a little more to rent many of these items, as opposed to buying them outright, but the money you save in freight could be worth it. The exhibitor guide is full of deadlines for reserving these items, so be sure to make arrangements for them before you arrive at the show. Renting items last-minute will certainly blow up your budget.

"If you need to add something bright and attractive in your booth that you don't want to ship, try buying some gorgeous live flowers in a vase right before the show. They should last the four to five days and can be disposed of, or given away, afterward."
—*Carolyn Edlund, ArtsyShark.com*

Hard Cards is a small greeting card company owned by Randi Picarelli and Stacey Rifkin. They are based in Los Angeles and are annual exhibitors at the National Stationery Show. The first year they exhibited, they purchased all their supplies in LA and shipped their entire booth cross-country to the tune of several hundred dollars. When the pallet arrived on their freight target date, several pieces of furniture had been damaged in transit and were completely unusable. They spent the night before opening day rushing around New York replacing and reconfiguring their entire booth. You can only imagine how stressful and exhausting that was!

Continued...

At their post-show debriefing, they realized it would have been less expensive to rent a few pieces from the show's decorating company, and then fly to New York a day early and buy whatever else they needed. Now they sketch out their booth in Los Angeles, research local suppliers in New York, and make arrangements for purchase, pick-up or delivery before they even board the plane. On their assigned day, they walk their booth into the Javits Center and start putting things together. After the show, they give away the furniture, much to the delight of local vendors and many New Yorkers!

This may not be the best way for you to put your booth together, but it is an excellent example of being creative in how you get your supplies to the exhibition hall.

Setting up Your Booth

Even though booth setup is technically something that happens during the show, we are including some information about it in the pre-show section to help give you a sense of what to expect.

One of the most nerve-wracking mistakes an exhibitor can make is not allowing enough time for booth setup. We have seen dozens of first-time exhibitors show up at noon on Saturday to start setting up their booths for a 9 a.m. opening the following day. Miraculously, many of them are able to pull it off, but they often look a little worse for wear.

If you can swing it, we really recommend being in place to begin setup as soon as your freight target date allows. Do everything you can to build in a time buffer for when things go wrong. It is always better to finish early than to be gluing cards onto a display board at 11 p.m. the night before the show opens.

"The best moment was setting up my entire booth in one day and having the next day (which was the day before the show started) to relax, get a haircut, and watch a movie! If you can, try to keep the day before the show as stress-free as possible. It really made a difference in terms of my overall mood going into the show."
—*Joyce Wan, Wanart*

While we are on the topic, consider giving yourself at least one extra day at the end of your trip too. Trust us when we say you do not want to be that person who tries to pack up their booth and rush to the airport an hour after the show closes. Most shows do not let you store your empty shipping containers inside your booth because they pose a fire hazard. Show management usually puts the containers into storage and will bring them out after the show closes. Among hundreds of other exhibitors' boxes, yours could take hours to arrive, which makes your departure time pretty unpredictable.

"You never know how long you might have to wait for your boxes to show up at the end of a show. The first show I did, I waited 30 minutes for my stuff. The next show, I waited seven hours."
—*Michael Caulder, Nuk-u-lur Greetings*

Setup days are one of the most glorious sights of controlled chaos you will ever witness. Boxes fly, tempers flare, laughter ensues, and a few tears may even flow. In the end, the empty and barren shell of the convention center transforms into a bright, colorful, vibrant and energetic environment. It really is fantastic to watch—and with a little planning, it can actually be fun and unpredictable too.

"I [arrived for] set up and I look at the booth next to mine. I realized that she has the same IKEA curtains that I do. Right next to me! The exact same curtains that I have as their backdrop!"
—*Megan Auman, megan auman*

"One year during set up, I fell through a wall and into a neighboring booth. I was so shocked, I just sat on the floor yelling, 'I've fallen! I've fallen into the booth!' over and over again. It was really funny. Fortunately, everything was okay, including me"
—*Amy Smyth, Amy Smyth Made It*

Be sure to bring all your show paperwork with you—contracts, rental agreements, shipping information, and receipts for anything you have booked in advance. This way you have a record of what you signed up for with you in the event of any setup issues or miscommunications.

"I exhibited at a show that claimed I didn't order my electricity in advance. I had my confirmation email proving that I had. Good thing, too, because otherwise I would have had to pay the on-site rate, which was WAY more expensive." —*Rob Fortier, Paper Words*

Your Toolbox

Simply having a well-stocked toolbox that contains the following items can eliminate much of your setup frustration:

- Screwdrivers (Phillips- and flat-head)
- Small hammer
- Wrench
- Electrical ties (zip ties)
- Binder clips (they have many uses)
- Scotch tape
- Heavy-duty tape (such as gaffer's tape)
- Self-adhesive Velcro
- Adhesive foam tape
- Safety pins
- First aid supplies
- Trash bags
- Extension cord
- Power strip
- Packing tape
- Portable steamer (if you are using curtains)
- Box cutter
- 3M Command Strips (for easy, no-damage hanging)

You may not use everything on this list, but, like a Boy Scout, be prepared. Plus, you can bet someone will need to borrow something. What better way to kick off a show than by making friends and being able to help out the exhibitors around you?

"The best part of set up is when the booth is done and you stand back and look at it... then, you go home and go to bed."
—*Randi Picarelli, Hard Cards*

We realize this is only a snapshot of all that goes in to putting your booth together. The good news is that there are many, many resources available to help. As we mentioned earlier, check out the books, blogs and websites designed especially to help young and first-time exhibitors. Reach out to more seasoned exhibitors with questions too; do this early—they are going to be busy getting ready for the show as well.

There are hard deadlines established by trade shows for shipping and supply requests. These are generally about six weeks before the show; so we recommend starting with your booth planning and design first. Once your booth is safely on its way, you can use the weeks directly leading up to the show to focus in on the rest of your pre-show plan.

So, how do you do that? Don't worry because we've got you covered. In the next chapter, we will help you get your company in the best position possible for press, sales reps and industry contacts—and we will have you looking good, too.

CHAPTER

4

Roll Out Your Pre-Show Plan

Now that your booth is, for the most part, finished, it is time to get your show momentum going. By now, you are familiar with the show rules and regulations, so you should not get in (too much) trouble. The Production Calendar has been keeping you on track and (mostly) sane. You have framed your plan of attack with realistic, attainable goals, and made the business decisions to back it all up. You also have some ideas of what to expect once you get to the show. So you can fully take advantage of your time on the floor, let's begin to incorporate customers, reps and the media in your quest to make trade-show success a reality.

Publicity

Just as you would not throw a party without sending invitations, don't just show up to a trade show and hope that people will find you. Devote some time and energy to making the industry aware of your presence before the show opens. This can be just as important as what you do at the show itself. It is easy to think you do not need any pre-show marketing and that people will find your awesome booth just by walking by. While this may be true, think about what could happen if they knew about you before the show and actually planned on stopping by? This is where the power of pre-show publicity comes in.

Press Releases

Companies usually send press releases when they debut new products. A press release is a document that is issued to the media, and announces your company, your products and related events. Media outlets, especially industry magazines, are constantly in need of content and rely heavily on press releases to fill in or generate stories.

Where do you think all the featured product pictures you see in the magazines originate? They come from press releases that are sent in by companies just like yours. Good magazine editors are incredibly knowledgeable about their fields, but they cannot be everywhere; they count on companies feeding them story leads and information. If you are debuting at a show or are releasing new products, send out a press release.

A press release should answer the Basic Five Questions: Who, What, When, Where, and Why. While there is a standard press release format (WebWire. com has a great template you can follow), different magazines may have different requirements, so be sure to find out the specific submission guidelines of each publication.

Websites and magazines will often reprint your release word for word, so it needs to be well written and newsworthy. Your statement should also be interesting to read. "Furry Pet Greetings debuting at the Locklear Trade Show in Saskatchewan" is a little flat. But how about "Furry Pet Greetings, a U.S.-based greeting card line featuring the fur of real pets, is making its Canadian debut at the Locklear Trade Show in Saskatchewan. Ten percent of all sales will be donated to the Canadian Humane Society." See the difference?

Whatever your niche, use it to make your press release interesting and readable. You are in a creative field, so use that talent! If writing is not your strong suit, find someone to help you. The important thing is that you take advantage of this opportunity to promote your company. To see an example of a press release, visit the Downloads section at www.CenterAisleGroup.com.

Your press release should also include high-resolution images of your products. Getting a write-up about your product is good; having your product featured visually and in full color is great!

Do your research and send your release to the correct editor. Many magazines have more than one and, unlike the old days, the editors do not necessarily work out of the same office. Your misdirected press release may just be deleted. Most of this information can easily be found on the magazine's website. If you are not sure, call or email to confirm the right editor.

Why go through all this trouble when you have 5,000 other details to attend to? FREE PUBLICITY. It is so important we are going to repeat it... FREE PUBLICITY!

We hate to ruin your feel-good fantasy, but Tiffany is the only celebrity who was randomly discovered at a suburban shopping mall food court and catapulted to stardom. Stars become stars not just because they have talent, but because they know how to get in front of the people who can help them grow their careers. As a trade show exhibitor, the people who can help you grow your business are the trade show attendees.

Most attendees read industry magazines, which are often sent out in advance of the show opening. Many of the industry publications will do special issues focused around major trade shows. Getting placement in these magazines is a great way to get the attention of potential buyers. These publications are usually distributed at shows for free. If a buyer missed reading about you before the show, they may notice your information while flipping through a magazine during their lunch break at the show or even after they get home. That is a lot of opportunity for exposure you can access for free.

Some great industry magazines to include in your press release distribution list are:

- GREETINGS etc., **www.greetings.edgl.com**
- Stationery Trends, **www.stationerytrendsmag.com**
- Gifts & Decorative Accessories, **www.giftsanddec.com**
- Giftware News, **www.giftwarenews.com**
- GIFT SHOP Magazine, **www.giftshopmag.com**

There are also dozens of blogs that write about stationery and gift lines; be sure to keep them in the loop. Don't overlook non-industry magazines, such as bridal, lifestyle and even fashion magazines. They always need content too, and you never know what story ideas the editors may be working on.

Magazines will often put out a call for product information and ask show management to contact all the exhibitors. Pay special attention to any email the show sends out about publicity opportunities. Be aware that press deadlines occur months prior to a magazine's release, especially if the magazine is only published quarterly.

Remember our friend the exhibitor guide? Be sure to check it for additional pre-show publicity suggestions from the show management.

Press Kits

Part of your pre-show planning should include preparing a press kit. Trade shows usually have a press room for exhibitors, which provide an excellent opportunity for more publicity. You do not need to go overboard with the number of press kits you have on hand. Generally, 25 to 30 kits will be sufficient.

A press room is exactly what it sounds like: a room where members of the press go to gather information about the show and its exhibitors. The show management provides space for each exhibitor to leave prepared press kits. The kits can be as simple as a folder with a product image and company information on the front. It should include a press release, images of your product and contact info. Besides a simple folder, you can get creative with the format and packaging of your release if the press room has space for something more elaborate. Just be sure to check with the show management in advance. Even having a simple presence in the press room gives you another chance for free publicity. Don't forget to include your booth number in case members of the press want to interview you.

Keep a few press kits in your booth as well to give to any member of the press who stop by to ask questions. You can easily hand them a kit rather than risk losing their attention and interest by sending them off to the press room to seek one out.

Other Publicity Opportunities

Many shows run contests for new products or innovative designs. Even if you think your product is not a prize-winning item, enter these contests anyway. Displays featuring all participants are placed in a prominent spot, often right at the show entrance where buyers can easily find them. These contests are a great opportunity for more free publicity.

Do not forget to use the power of social media on the show floor as well. Most trade shows create hash tags for trending on Twitter. Find them and use them so others can easily follow your updates. If you have a laptop or smartphone, update your feeds to let people know what's going on in your booth. Post updates about sales you've just made, cool people you have met, any activities or demonstrations going on in your booth, or show specials for those following you online at the show. If you are really fancy, you can upload pictures and even video of your booth happenings too. Just be sure to include your booth number in your updates; your brilliant content will not be of much use if no one knows where your booth is located.

Set up Face Time

Get a jumpstart on meeting—or even exceeding—your show goals before the first day. Look at the list of new stores and new reps you want to secure and the industry people you want to meet. Start the ball rolling by setting up show appointments with these people in advance.

Do not be concerned about appearing desperate or overeager by calling in advance for a show appointment. The earlier you make contact the better, since retailers, reps and other industry people are just as busy as you getting ready for a show.

Calling or emailing your prospective show appointments early actually works to your advantage. Show days can be very busy for attendees and schedules fill up quickly. Asking to set up a meeting time well in advance will help secure your spot on the calendar. Trying to schedule meetings less than two weeks before a show will probably not result in much success. It also might leave your invitee wondering why you are waiting until the last minute.

Setting up show appointments does not have to be a big, formal event. You can simply call or email to extend the invitation. If you send an email, be sure to include a link to your website or even a PDF of your catalog. Plan on following up with a phone call, too. Buyers are flooded with email—and spam filters can be merciless. You do not want to miss out just because you did not follow up.

We encourage you to set up a specific day and time, but do not be surprised if some people are not willing to commit and just promise to stop by during the show. Do not take this personally. Show time is prime time for attendees, who often have very full agendas.

Who are some of the people you want to meet with?

Retailers. There are probably retailers in your address book that you would love to have carry your line. These may be prospective accounts or customers who have ordered from you in the past but have gone dormant. Why not extend a personal invitation to them to visit your booth during the show? Reach out to them and set up an appointment at the show to introduce them to your new designs or look at the line for the first time.

Sales Reps. Take advantage of being under the same roof as many of the prospective reps for your line. Before you contact them, take some time to learn about the kinds of lines they rep and if they are even appropriate for your company. If you can, try to find out if they are picking up any new lines. Some reps are always looking for new lines; others are not.

Meeting with reps at a trade show is a great way to showcase your line in its entirety as well as introduce new designs to your existing reps. It is also a good opportunity to get feedback on ways to improve your line, your sales materials or your fulfillment processes.

You might be wondering what input a rep could possibly have about your creative brilliance and the answer is simple: reps work with retailers every day. No one knows what is happening on the front lines better than the sales reps who are slinging the products. You may not always agree with what they have to say, and they may not always be right, but the conversation could be interesting and insightful nonetheless.

"Listen to what everyone is saying and then make changes. It's hard but don't resist it. Don't take things so personally and if you don't know what someone is talking about, just say so."
—Amy Smyth, Amy Smyth Made It.

Many new and young card companies have big ideas about exhibiting at a show and signing up a nation-wide sales force in four short days. Unfortunately, this does not always happen. We will discuss reps in more detail in Part 2; but do keep in mind that if you are a new company, you may get some resistance from reps. Again, do not take this personally.

Experienced, productive reps are in high demand and many are simply at maximum capacity in terms of manufacturers. They may also be hesitant to sign up with a new business. In our experience, most greeting card and gift companies are not prepared to hire outside sales reps for the first twelve to eighteen months of being in business. Do not be discouraged by this. In the early stages, the success of your business does not hinge on having an outside sales force. There is so much you can do on your own. Use this time as an opportunity to develop your line more fully and get your company truly rep ready. Just keep doing what you are already doing; the reps will come when the timing is right.

Industry People. There may be industry people you want to meet during the show, such as suppliers, vendors, sales managers, consultants and other manufacturers. And just like with reps and retailers, having everyone together under one roof is a golden opportunity to make connections. Whether your agenda is to get a better deal on envelopes or just to introduce yourself, take advantage of the access to these people that a show provides.

Industry Experts. In addition to providing a unique chance to grow your business numbers and your network, most trade shows also offer opportunities to grow your business smarts. Make a point of investigating the education track for buyers and exhibitors and registering for some of the sessions. These are terrific opportunities to advance your professional development by learning from other people in the industry. Some of these workshops are held before the show and can be very helpful as you prepare to exhibit. Not all of the sessions will apply to you, but take the time to investigate the offerings as you put your show plan together, especially if the pre-show workshops will mean arriving on site a day early.

There is a great deal of work that happens behind the scenes and way before your booth gets set up. Take full advantage of the opportunities that trade shows provide to help your company be at its best going into the show. The possibilities are endless!

Getting Yourself Ready: Looking and Feeling Fabulous

"It's really exciting when the booth is up. It's done and it's up, and it's like my stage. Now what am I going to wear? It has to match my booth—I can't clash with it!" —*Suzanne Karlson, Lumia Designs*

You've invested a lot of time and money into making your booth look great and getting your company into top form. Now it is time to think about you looking great. Just like your booth gives an impression of your line and your company, so does your wardrobe and appearance.

Generally, the days of suits and ties are gone. You will still see some exhibitors and attendees wearing them, but for the most part, trade shows have become a business-casual environment. We are not going to explore what "business casual" means here. If you are not sure, we encourage you to investigate the hundreds of fashion websites or books available through your local, independently owned bookstore.

Basically, you are going to want to look sharp but still be comfortable. As of this writing, jeans seem to be more acceptable on the floor, provided they are clean, well fitting, without holes and paired with a nicer shirt. You will definitely encounter differing opinions on this but we include it because we suspect you're wondering. The bottom line is that trade show days are long; tight, restrictive clothing, worn for the purposes of looking professional, will only make them seem longer.

The same goes for shoes. For years we have marveled at the women who work the show floor in high heels. They look terrific and have our utmost respect but we still vote for comfortable, broken-in shoes with good arch support. Ask anyone who works in a hospital or grocery store about the importance of practical footwear. Meryl is an undercover (and uncompensated) spokesperson for Dansko clogs and Rob swears by Rockport.

You might be wondering why we are making such a big deal about clothes and footwear. Quite simply, we want to save you the agony of our past mistakes. Getting a blister from those cute new shoes on the first day is going to make the rest of the week very uncomfortable.

"Dress in a way that's in line with your company image. Look like your product. No matter what, be willing to wear comfortable shoes." —*Randi Picarelli, Hard Cards*

Your outfit can be an extension of your booth design, too. Many companies dress in matching shirts that play off the colors of the booth or wear hats that may grab a buyer's attention. Costumes can be appropriate, too, for the right companies. Just remember not to have a gimmick so big that it overshadows your product or hinders order writing.

Several years ago, we saw a first-time exhibitor at a trade show who had a huge double booth filled with floor plants and with dance music playing. The front of the booth was lined with a long table piled up with beads, stickers and catalogs; the rest of the booth was filled with buff, shirtless men and drag queens. It was definitely one of the most fun and lively booths that year.

Unfortunately, the show was a total bust for them. The booth was so busy and chaotic that buyers did not know what the exhibitor was actually selling. Order writing was completely hindered by all the activity in the booth. It just so happens that this was a greeting card line. The cards were displayed along the back wall, but all the people crowding the booth—not the least of whom were the seven-foot-tall drag queens—made it impossible to see the product at all. The drag queens, while amazing, were really intimidating to half the buyers, and the buff, shirtless men scared the other half away.

This is not to say you should not be creative or even outrageous with your booth or your costume. Some of the shows could use a little outrageousness. But this is not performance art. The point of exhibiting is to make your product and the selling of that product the focus of your booth.

"I always bring warm clothes, comfortable shoes and a bag that rolls. My suitcase is a basic businessman bag that isn't arty or creative at all and I don't care. It just makes it easy to roll down the street." —*Amy Smyth, Amy Smyth Made It*

Get in Sellin' Shape

It is no secret that trade shows are hard work, both mentally and physically. As you get your booth ready to exhibit, take some time to get yourself ready too.

This may seem unrealistic, especially as you go into that last 10-day crunch time, but make taking care of yourself a priority. We cannot emphasize strongly enough the importance of not rolling into a trade show exhausted, dehydrated and generally compromised. Not only will you not be at your physical and mental best, but you will run the risk of getting sick after you get home, if not before.

You might be thinking, "That's nice, but I'm already pretty healthy." While that may be true, trade shows require a level of stamina and energy that most of us do not use as we execute our daily lives. Give yourself an advantage by adding a little pre-show tune-up to your preparation plan.

Power Up. For two weeks before the show, drink eight ounces of water with a packet of Emergen-C every day. This little pack supplements your vitamins and helps boost your immune system, which will be taxed big time between the travel and the sheer volume of human contact you are about to encounter. Do this even if you already take a multivitamin. You can get these in individual packets or boxes at most health food, grocery and drug stores as well as online.

We are not doctors; nor do we play them on television. We are not compensated for our celebrity endorsement of this product, either. Nonetheless, this is what works for us, and years of trade shows have made it a must-have in our travel kits.

Hydrate. Along with your vitamin boost, make an extra effort to get properly hydrated before the show. Hopefully, this is already part of your daily routine. Regardless, it will go a long way to helping you keep up when the physical rigors of the show kick in.

Sleep! We know all about the temptation to stay up late as deadlines approach. With a comprehensive production schedule, this should be avoidable. Still, it is important that you get enough sleep every night of the week leading up to the show. We have found turning in just an hour earlier makes a significant difference.

Eat Well. Go easy on your food heading into a show, too. The combination of improper eating, fatigue and dehydration is a powder keg waiting to go off. Be mindful of eating healthy, balanced meals as you head into show week.

Build Some Stamina. In the two weeks leading up to the show, be sure to get to the gym or keep participating in whatever fitness routine you have. If you do not have one, consider starting one—now! Not only will exercise help manage your stress, but you will be less fatigued during the show as well as after.

If you are not used to standing and walking from place to place all day and all of a sudden you go from zero to 60, your body is going to have trouble keeping up. Start building the physical stamina necessary to keep your "A" game in place. It doesn't matter if it is a full-on workout or a walk around the block; just do something to get your body primed.

Comforts of Home

If you are traveling for a trade show, it is important to bring some of the comforts of home with you for your hotel room so that you feel, well, comfortable.

Travel, especially for a show, puts your whole routine, including your eating and sleeping schedules, out of whack. Here are some items you may want to bring with you to make yourself at home.

- Your bathrobe and slippers
- Earplugs and an eye mask (if you are a light sleeper)
- Emergen-C or vitamins
- Music to relax with
- A book to read
- Your favorite tea to enjoy in your room

While you don't want to over-pack, anything you can bring that will help you relax and recharge at the end of the day is worth it. We will address self-care while at the show in more detail in Part 2.

By now, you may be thinking: this is all well and good, but when do you start writing orders and making money? Well, much of the big wheeling and dealing is going to happen at the show itself. But what happens once you actually arrive on site? How do you behave and, more importantly, what do you say to buyers when they come into your booth? In the next section, we will examine booth etiquette and look at strategies for connecting with buyers and making sales.

PART TWO | # During The Show

CHAPTER 5

Basic Show and Booth Etiquette

"Try to have fun. Try to sell cards. Try not to stress out too much."
—*Lauren Gryniewski, Old Tom Foolery*

It's showtime! After weeks, months or possibly years of preparing, it is time to hit the floor. This is your chance to shine and be a star. Just like with any production, you are going to want to give the performance of your life— especially if this is your big debut.

For many first- and even second- or third-time exhibitors, the show floor can be an intimidating place. It is not unusual to feel overshadowed by, or even inadequate next to, some of the large, elaborate booths filled with professional, polished looking staff. So much work has gone into just getting here that it is easy to feel added pressure for the investment to pay off. How do you deflate some of that pressure?

To start with, understand that trade shows are not just about writing orders and getting new customers. While these are important aspects of exhibiting, some of the most valuable benefits of trade shows come from all the things that happen when you are not writing orders. Remember, the actual exhibiting is not the end, but just one step in the trade show process.

Perhaps most importantly, exhibiting at trade shows provides the invaluable opportunity to meet and start real-time relationships with people in the industry: suppliers, artists, other manufacturers, customers, prospects, sales reps and industry leaders. Oh and, of course, celebrities like us!

We have countless stories about manufacturers who have made industry connections that have saved them money, and retail connections that have made them money, as a direct result of meeting at a trade show. Keep in mind that some of your best show dealings may happen in the weeks and months after the show is over. We will discuss this more in Part 3.

It is also important to recognize the intangible value of a booth. It not only provides the unique opportunity to present your line in all of its glory, but it also gives you a chance to see how your products fit into the larger industry. You can see what other manufacturers are creating as well as get a visual sense of trends, colors, design styles and general happenings in a way that is difficult, if not impossible, to get anywhere else.

You may be rolling your eyes and thinking this is a pretty abstract reason to invest a couple of thousand dollars and hundreds of hours of work. On the surface, you are correct. You could just walk the show and glean that kind of information... or could you?

Exhibiting is an immersive process. After a week of setup, staffing your booth, talking to retailers, reps and other manufacturers, it is almost impossible not to walk away with more first-hand knowledge and a deeper understanding of how an industry works. All the workshops, blogs and books in the world (including this one) are no substitution for actually jumping in there and getting your hands dirty.

But we digress...

One area that many exhibitors have the most questions about is show and booth etiquette. We are not referring to just following show rules here. Even though etiquette can be a pretty stuffy-sounding word, how you behave in your booth at the show will make a big difference in your show outcome. If you have ever attended a trade show before, you have probably seen a wide spectrum of booth behavior. Depending upon the industry, that behavior may or may not have been appropriate. So, assuming you are at a mainstream type of show, how do you behave?

The Basics of Booth and Floor Behavior

Be Friendly. A big part of exhibiting at trade shows is just being friendly to both the people walking past your booth and the manufacturers in the surrounding booths. It also means being available to answer questions. Some of those questions will be about your product line and some will be about where the nearest ice cream cart can be found. After a couple of hours of directing people to ice cream, you may start to feel a little frustrated that they are not asking you about your line. Regardless of the type of interaction, keep your show face on and be nice to everyone, especially other exhibitors.

Have Respect. In days past, some exhibitors were not always so nice to one another—and some still aren't. Be cool and be polite, even if their product is similar to yours. As you walk around the show, you may see products you want to look at up close. To enter another exhibitor's booth, it is protocol to wait to be invited or to ask the exhibitor for permission to enter.

To first-time participants, such a rule may seem harsh and totally unfriendly but it is in place for a reason. Many long-time trade show exhibitors have astonishing stories of competing manufacturers marching in and blatantly taking pictures, making sketches of new designs and generally behaving badly in their booths. We do not tell you this to scare you or instill paranoia; just be aware of this history and err on the side of respect and caution.

"You can't buy anything that's on display [in other manufacturer's booths]! When we went to [a show] to scope out the scene, we immediately headed to the [booth of a manufacturer we love] and starting grabbing up all the things we wanted to buy. We had to be put in our place by the guy working their booth, which was really embarrassing. I'm not sure what we were thinking."
—*Joel Gryniewski, Old Tom Foolery*

Be Social. Not every minute of the day will have you hustling around your booth answering questions about your line and scribbling down orders at lightning speed. Expect to have some downtime and plan to make the most of it. When it is quiet, take some time to talk to and get to know the other exhibitors around you. This is a priceless opportunity to build a network of people who you can help and who can, possibly, help you. We know of several exhibitors who have picked up reps or discovered better printing deals as a result of on-the-floor conversations with other exhibitors.

Making friends early on is a really good idea for several reasons: first, hanging out with your new friends will make your days much more entertaining; second, many returning exhibitors get assigned the same booth space with the same neighbors year after year, and that is one way long-term industry relationships get formed. Who knows what could be in store for you and your company.

"I'm lucky because I've had a lot of good show neighbors that have taken me under their wing." —*Megan Auman, megan auman*

Friendship has its limits though. If you are in a conversation with your neighbor, and a customer comes into either booth, break off the conversation and get to the customer. Do not worry about being polite to your fellow exhibitor in this case. You are both there to sell your products and everyone will understand if you have to leave the conversation—except the buyer if you ignore them! Be mindful that you do not block the front of your booth—or other booths, for that matter. Just step off to the side.

There may be times when large groups of buyers will congregate in front of your booth, blocking everything. For the most part, be cool about this. Having people in and around your booth is a good thing. Booths with people in them tend to attract more people. However, if you notice they are preventing customers from accessing your booth, politely ask them to step over to the side. Chances are they are completely unaware of the fact that they are blocking your booth.

Stand and Deliver. While in your booth, stand as much as possible and keep busy. Even though most of the setup has already been done, there are always things to organize, re-sort and redisplay, especially after a busy rush of buyer activity. Reorganizing your sample decks or rearranging a disheveled display is a great way to pass the time, and will probably be necessary anyway. Arrange your cards by occasion, bestsellers, or price point. Use downtime to finish writing up orders, process leads to be followed up on, or add prospects into your database. Update your social media feeds with positive "from the floor" updates, too. Just be aware of people coming into your booth or expressing interest in your line.

"You can't be on your feet all day so take a director's chair with you to the show. This will keep you at eye level with show attendees even though you are seated." —*Carolyn Edlund, ArtsyShark.com*

"Bring a computer. You need that for down time, especially on [the last day] when you want to shoot yourself. I use it to update my database, check my email, and keep my business going. I will also research prospects before they come back to help them better"
    —*Amy Smyth, Amy Smyth Made It*

"Nothing looks worse than having your booth manned by someone just sitting in a folding chair and not being really attentive. They look like they don't care." —*Barbara Wade, Indigo Paper Goods*

Mind the 'Tude, Dude. There is nothing less inspiring than a bored, uninterested, counting-down-the-minutes-to-closing-time exhibitor. Please do not sit on a stool in the corner with your face buried in a newspaper, a book, or locked on a computer screen the entire time. Building industry connections and a customer base is difficult if you are hanging out on Facebook snarking about how slow the show is or lamenting the fact that you are not writing any orders.

It is important to keep a positive attitude about being at the show, even if you are not as busy as you would like. Maintain your excitement about your line—or at least be able to fake it well. It can get really disappointing when hours go by and you have not written any orders. Please do not let this discourage you. Having confidence in your product is so important. How can you expect prospective customers or potential sales reps to believe in your product if you don't?

"At the show, I just try to remain positive and perky and ignore the bitterness and crabbiness around me. And, I always try to be as accommodating as possible." —*Amy Smyth, Amy Smyth Made It*

It will not take long for you to meet plenty of people who spend more time complaining about trade shows than seeing them for the golden opportunities they are. If we had a dime for every time we asked someone in the aisles how it was going and they sarcastically replied, "Well, you know, I'm here," we would be retired! That kind of negative attitude leads to a very long week.

If someone ever replied, "Things are good. Orders are a little slow, but I'm so excited to be here!" we would probably pass out; then, we would jump up and hug them. See the difference in the mindset? Get your head on straight and be aware of how you answer the question, "How's it going?"

Honestly, there will be times when your booth or even your entire aisle is empty. You may find that you are nowhere near your sales goals or that you have not written any orders at all. That can be disheartening and discouraging. As difficult as it may be to find the positive, we really encourage you to make the best of the situation and look for opportunities to make your show a success in other ways. Remember all of your show goals, not just those involving money.

Even if everyone around you is in the same boat, do not gripe and complain to your neighbors. Quite frankly, no one wants to hear it. Rather than complaining, find something to do that keeps you active. Use that time to get caught up on post-show administrative work or even other aspects of your business. Who knows, seeing all your line on full display might inspire you to create a whole new collection!

Cell Phones. Be aware of how and when to use your cell phone. Do not sit in the booth and talk on your phone for hours on end. At a recent show, we saw an exhibitor talking on her phone in the booth. A buyer came in and was looking at her line. The exhibitor covered the phone with her hand, looked at the buyer and said, "Just let me know if you have any questions"—at which point she went back to the phone conversation! We are not making this up. Needless to say, the buyer was equally flabbergasted and left the booth without another word and without placing an order. Our guess is that buyer will never order from that manufacturer based on this single incident, and we're not sure we blame him.

Eating. Think carefully before eating a full-on lunch spread in your booth. Munching on a handful of nuts or drinking a beverage is one thing, but eating a drippy salad, overstuffed sandwich or smelly Chinese take-out is simply poor form. Prospective buyers or sales reps are, generally, not comfortable interrupting lunch. Not only that, but trying to talk to someone who's still chewing on a bite of Caesar salad is just gross (not to mention unprofessional).

"As long as I have lip gloss and water, I'm good."
—*Barbara Wade, Indigo Paper Goods*

Everyone needs to take a break at some point. If you are in your booth alone, just post a sign saying "Back in 10 minutes" and tell your neighbor, with whom you are now friendly, that you will be right back. Then, step out of your booth to eat. Ideally, you already have your food with you and do not have to go wait in the long concession lines, but we will get to that in a minute.

Beware: Prize Pigs

If you decided to have a giveaway, be advised that there is an upside, and a downside, to this practice. The upside, of course, is that everyone who takes your pen/notepad/button will have a way of remembering your booth number, your company name and possibly your product itself. Giveaways can serve as a great point of entry for talking to buyers, especially if you have a gimmick associated with them. People will almost always ask if they may have one of whatever it is you have on your front table, and you can have lots of fun with this.

The obvious answer to their question is, "of course," but think about some of the creative ways you can use that question to engage the buyer. Try changing your response from "Sure" to "Yes, but you have to tell me your name; I need more friends. I'm Janet and my line is Furry Pet Greetings." Some people will not play along, and that's fine. Others will have a great sense of humor about it—and who knows where that might lead!

And now the downside: Bear in mind that every trade show also has its fair share of what we affectionately call "prize pigs." These are attendees who gobble up all the candy, catalogs, buttons and plastic tchotchkes they can stuff into a bag, never to be heard from again. Accept that you will encounter these people and let it go before you even leave home.

"The minute I see [prize pigs] are just in my booth for the free sample I try to get them out of my booth as quickly and as politely as possible. That's part of learning how to qualify your prospects and spending your time and energy on actual prospective buyers."
—*Joyce Wan, Wanart*

Get in the mindset of your freebie being just that—free. You will do yourself a big favor from the beginning by writing off the giveaway before you even open the box. Do not get bent if someone takes your freebie and walks away without even acknowledging you, your line, or the fact that you have a big, beautiful (and expensive) booth. Trade shows often bring out everyone's inner eight year old. Who can really resist a table loaded up with free anything—especially candy!

One way of bypassing prize pigs and possibly making your giveaways more valuable is to reserve your freebies for customers who place orders, sort of like a free gift with purchase. Simply put your treasures at the back of your booth or hidden under a table and not in the front within easy access. When someone places an order, say thank you and let them know you have a special gift for them; then simply pull out one gift for each buyer in the party, even if only one person placed the order. They may not all take you up on it, but you will look like a champ for offering.

Taking Care of Yourself

We talked about pre-show self-care in the previous section, and looking after yourself shouldn't stop once you get on site. Taking care of yourself while exhibiting at a trade show is extremely important. No matter how busy your life at home might be, chances are your time at the show will tap the deepest of your mental, physical and creative reserves. If you implemented a pre-show training program, keep it going during the show. If you did not, you can still take steps to take care of yourself during a show run.

Clear Your Head. After standing on your feet all day, the last thing you want to do is walk back to your hotel, especially if there is a comfortable shuttle bus waiting outside. If your hotel is within half a mile of the convention center, do yourself a favor and walk back. Use this time to clear your head and breath some fresh air. Trust us on this.

Reduce the Pain. You can help ward off puffy feet and achy legs by taking a good anti-inflammatory, such as ibuprophen. Take a dose every night and another dose in the morning. Again, we are not doctors. However, we have found this helps reduce the swelling in our feet and legs as well as ward off the general aches and pains that come from standing for long hours at a time.

Stay Sober. Yes, sober. Do not drink any alcohol until the last day of the show—this includes the night before the show opens. We like, and often need, a nightcap as much as anyone; but hours in a convention center with recycled air, as well as the inevitable sodium-laden foods, will bring on unimaginable levels of dehydration. There is no need to aid that process. Besides, you want to be alert and sharp at the show.

Power Up. Just as you did in the weeks leading up to the show, give your immune system a boost by continuing to take your vitamins, supplements and Emergen-C during the show. The FDA may not have proven its effectiveness, but it works for us.

Hydrate. We cannot emphasize enough the importance of water, or the importance of anticipating lines at the restrooms. Staying hydrated also means going easy on caffeine. This does not mean you should abandon your morning coffee or soda altogether; it just means that while you may be tempted to have an afternoon coffee or soft drink to perk you up, your fatigue may just be dehydration.

If you do not drink water during show hours, make sure you guzzle it down in the evenings. Every night on your way back to your hotel, pick up one or two one-liter bottles or get a bottle the first day and refill it. Just make sure you drink it down before you go to sleep. Be sure to pick up an extra bottle to take with you to the show venue, too, and avoid those higher convention center prices.

Stay Focused. You are here to work, so limit your evening activities—even if it is your first time in the host city. Bleary-eyed, zombie-faced exhibitors are not engaging exhibitors. It is very important that you do not over-schedule yourself with non-show activities. If you want to see the city, go back on a vacation or use the extra day you scheduled in during your show preparations.

You may have the opportunity to go out in the evenings with buyers or other exhibitors you meet. By all means do this! Just keep an eye on the clock so you can still get your beauty sleep.

Eat Well. We are both big foodies and love rich, indulgent meals. While we certainly appreciate and encourage the celebratory meal at the end, keep your eating in check during the show. It is very easy to fall victim to the convenience of a street vendor or the convention center food court.

If at all possible, pack yourself a day's worth of food in an insulated lunch bag and take it with you. Most restaurants and delis that serve breakfast will also have sandwiches ready to grab and go, or you can order one. Another option is to have mini-meals throughout the day, such as fresh fruit, nuts, liquid meal replacements (such as Orgain), and nutrition bars. Many of these items can even be packed in your suitcase. Depending on the location of the show, you may have access to a grocery store, convenience store or deli that will carry these items as well. The point is to avoid eating things high in sugar, sodium, guar gum, and any ingredients not found in nature.

More than likely, you will be dining out every evening, whether with your own crew or with people you meet at the show. Eat as early as possible and make careful food selections. Avoid those tempting, heavy, fatty foods and overeating out of exhaustion. Instead, choose dishes that are vegetable-laden, and broth or water-based soups. If you eat meat, go for lean cuts and watch your portions. You will be tired enough with the overall demands of the show, and there's no reason to add to the burden you are putting on your body.

Sleep! It is so important that you get enough sleep every night of the show, especially the night before the show opens. If you usually go to bed at 11 p.m., consider turning in at 10 p.m. and sleeping as late as possible without creating a panicked, crazy morning.

The Cast of Characters You Will Meet

The hustle and bustle of the show floor is exciting. There is a special thrill that comes from watching people walking around, meeting and greeting old friends, and looking at all the beautiful products—not to mention the snippets of gossip you will pick up as people pass your booth. But who are all these people? What do they do and what should you know about them?

There are eight primary types of show attendees: artists, buyers, licensees, distributors, importers, press, industry guests, and tourists. Your main interest, and most of your interaction, will be with buyers, but it is important to be aware of the other categories.

Artists. You may encounter fellow artists who attend the show, portfolio in hand, looking for manufacturers to license their work. As a new or young company, this is probably not something you will be interested in or ready for. Do not feel the least bit hesitant or guilty for saying "no," or "thanks, but I'm not interested." Artists are accustomed to being rejected; for them, trade shows can be worse than a night in a singles bar. You should feel comfortable talking to any artist that approaches your booth, but they can be a chatty bunch. Be careful not to spend too much time with them and possibly ignore potential retailers and reps.

There will, inevitably, be an artist who comes into your booth, notebook in hand, and looks admiringly and most studiously at your designs. They will then turn to you and say something like, "Wow. I'm so inspired to work on my own line now." Resist the urge to clobber them or threaten them with a lawsuit if they steal your ideas. Instead, tell them you are flattered and get a business card or their contact information. Offer to answer questions via email; they may be far less likely to copy you, no matter how inadvertently, if they know they are being watched.

Buyers. This is the primary category of show attendee that you, as an exhibitor, are most interested in, and we will discuss them in much more detail in the next chapter.

Licensees. Some manufacturers do not employ their own art staff. Instead, they contract with other companies or artists to use their artwork. These are called licensees.

The artist signs a contract that specifies the length of time the manufacturer can use the artwork and is paid either a flat fee and/or royalties based on product sales. Typically these contracts run from two to three years and may also specify what products the art can be used on. Artists can choose to sell their designs outright to a company, but in doing so they usually surrender all rights to the artwork.

"Our policy is that we always agree, even if we don't know what they're talking about. One year, we had someone come in and ask us if we did licensing. We immediately responded, 'Oh yeah, we do that!' Then, after they left the booth, we scrambled around learning everything we could about it in case they came back."
—*Amy Smyth, Amy Smyth Made It*

Many licensing agreements are not exclusive. It is possible for an artist to license the same designs simultaneously to one company that makes coffee mugs and to another company that makes T-shirts.

Distributors. Distributors are companies that buy products from a manufacturer in bulk. They house, resell and ship those products to retail stores. Distributors can be a great opportunity for new and young companies since they often sell smaller lines along with larger and more established ones. Just be aware that they often require steep discounts on wholesale prices.

Importers. Importers are companies that purchase items from companies based in one country to sell in another country. Some importers are also distributors. A U.S.-based distributor may import cards from England. Once inside the U.S., the cards are stored in a warehouse from which the importer packs and ships the products.

Press. As we mentioned in the previous chapter, you may see representatives from the media. All of the industry magazines, as well as some general publications, will have working press people at the major trade shows. They are looking for content about trends, and hot new products and manufacturers. It goes without saying that you should be nice to media people. They should be wearing badges that identify them as press. Feel free to ask for credentials or for clarification of use for any pictures that will be taken. Do not be shy about saying "no" to anyone you think is shady.

Industry Guests. Industry guests can be anyone from a non-exhibiting manufacturer to an industry consultant to someone invited to attend directly by show management. Most trade shows have expanded the registration categories and we have seen fewer guests in recent years.

Tourists. These are generally friends and family members of exhibitors and retailers. They most likely will be registered as staff of the attending or exhibiting company. For the most part, they just sort of harmlessly pose as industry people. Be friendly and personable to them if they come into your booth. It is not unusual for retailers to divide and conquer a show to save time; you don't want to lose a sale because you were rude to someone's mom who is out doing research on their behalf.

Some of these people may express an interest in purchasing one or two of your products or even offer to buy your samples at the end of the show. Have a stack of business cards to give out with your website listed so they can either buy from you online or find a local retailer.

Catalogs vs. Takeaways

You will be routinely asked if you have a catalog. We recommend giving a catalog to anyone who wants one, even to those booth visitors who seem like long shots. With that being said, catalog distribution is not a free-for-all.

When someone enters your booth and asks for a catalog, what do you say? We do not recommend giving them the suspicious eye, shining a light in their face and interrogating them. That is not an advisable way to make friends or gain customers, as you have probably guessed.

Instead, engage the person requesting the catalog as much as possible. Where are they from? What is the name of their store and what kind of store is it? What part of your line are they most interested in? Gather as much information as you can regarding what caught their attention about your line. Some buyers will not be responsive to even the most charming of attempts. Do not take this personally. We will discuss customer engagement more in the next chapter.

Before giving out a catalog, always ask for a business card. Many buyers will automatically hand one to you. This will allow you to keep a record of the prospect. Be sure to make notes on your conversation: do not rely on your memory. By the end of the day, you will have met so many people that the business cards will be meaningless to you without some kind of memory jog. Did you give the person a catalog? Talk about specific products? Bond over your love of reality TV? You will want this information when you, or your rep, contact the account after the show. You may not have a rep in that territory right now, but when you get one the information may prove helpful. You never know who will turn into a customer, or when you will need to gush about what happened on *Real Housewives* to a fellow enthusiast.

"We make very specific notes on the back of business cards we get at shows and include everything we might need to remember a customer. Sometimes it might say something like 'fat lady in tight jeans; has store in Massachusetts' or 'cranky lady in red sweater'. Whatever it takes to remember who they are."
    —*Randi Picarelli, Hard Cards*

Some buyers will run out of business cards, especially toward the end of the show; or they may have left their cards at home. Never fear! You can still collect the contact information in whatever data-collection method you chose during your pre-show planning—be it a scanner, a direct entry to your database or in a notebook. If you handwrite the information, make sure your writing is legible. Don't miss out on a sale because you did not take the time (or care) to write clearly and accurately.

"If someone talks to me briefly and I don't get a business card from them, I am the ultimate name-badge stalker. I have a whole running list of people I talked to, based on reading their name badge. Really, if I know the name of their store and the city they're in, I can look them up." —*Megan Auman, megan auman*

Not all buyers will want to take a catalog but will ask, instead, that one be sent to them after the show. The answer to that is, "Sure!" Your pre-show planning will already have that mailing date scheduled, so all you will need to do is prepare the mailing labels, right?

If you travel with a laptop and have it in your booth, why not have a label template open and ready? That way, you can prepare your catalog mailing labels during downtime in your booth instead of in a marathon session later. Then, when you get home, all you have to do is print, stick and mail the catalogs.

As we went over in Part 1, having catalogs available for distribution in your booth is an important element in your show success. Buyers have a limited amount of time, and most have a long list of things to get done and hundreds of exhibitors to look at. Buying teams will often split up to cover a show, and then review catalogs together later. Others want to review all their options before making commitments. Many buyers will pick up catalogs, go back to their hotel rooms at night and decide which booths to return to the next day to place orders. Others will collect catalogs and make ordering decisions in the weeks following the show. For many buyers, printed catalogs are still an important purchasing tool. Do not lose out just because you think they are not important.

How many catalogs you take to a trade show depends on the industry, the size of your company and the size of the show. Some companies will hand out 500 catalogs and others will give away 50. As a new or young company, we suggest taking 200 to 250 catalogs to a larger show, such as the National Stationery Show, and about half as many to a regional or local show. However many catalogs you bring, make sure your booth number is clearly listed on the front cover. You can add this with a simple sticker you print at home. If a buyer takes a catalog, make sure they can easily find your booth if they decide to place an order later on during the show.

There is no right or wrong answer to the "Who do you give a catalog to?" question; opinions vary depending on whom you ask. But we do not recommend standing at the edge of your booth handing out catalogs to everyone who walks past. As you get more experience exhibiting, you will be able to gauge the best way to pass out your catalogs; you will also develop a sense of who is a serious prospect and who is a prize pig.

"I'm not comfortable handing someone our body of work without knowing something about who they are. I want to make sure they go into the hands of buyers." —*Randi Picarelli, Hard Cards*

"I give out catalogs to anyone. That makes the sale. It makes no sense to me to protect your catalogs."
—*Amy Smyth, Amy Smyth Made It*

Takeaways. You will also encounter the occasional trade show browser who does not have a business card, does not want a catalog, and leaves you wondering if they are even in the right place. For them, we recommend having a takeaway, such as a postcard with your company name, logo, website and booth number. You may even want the postcard design to look the same as the front of your catalog, with all your contact information and booth number on the back. This is an easy and cost-effective giveaway that you can stack up on the table at the front of your booth next to your candy bowl.

As with other show giveaways, it is really important to understand going in that the majority of catalog pick-ups will just evaporate. Even the most enthusiastic booth visitor sometimes transforms into an unfriendly rain cloud after the show. Our experience has been that the most seasoned buyers will write orders at the show; new buyers or new stores will order within four weeks and the prize pigs will just disappear. We don't know why this happens, but accepting that it does will help avoid the post-show blues of thinking no one likes you. We will talk about some effective post-show follow-up techniques in Part 3.

Sales Reps

Just as buyers are looking for lines at trade shows, reps are often looking for lines, too. If you have set up appointments with sales reps ahead of time, or if a rep just stops by your booth, be prepared to talk to them about your line in their territory, which groups you work with, as well as which lines they carry.

"I think one year we had a 'reps wanted' icon in the directory, but usually we just talk to reps that stop by our booth. Sometimes we will get in touch with reps that we're interested in working with before the show and invite them to stop by our booth."
    —*Lauren Gryniewski, Old Tom Foolery*

Visiting with sales reps in your booth is a great way to get to know them and understand a little bit more about how they work. These conversations can be quite revealing about whether or not they are even the right rep for you. For instance, if your product is geared toward teenage girls, a rep who specializes in sporting goods and sports-related products might not be the best fit—even though lots of teenage girls play sports.

Be prepared to take time to really acquaint a potential rep with your line, but do not get your feelings hurt if they are not interested in your pitch. Some reps need time to take in your line, so step back and give them room to look at the samples and flip through your catalog. Others will be able to make snap decisions about whether or not a line is right for them.

If you are approached by a sales rep or group principal who is interested in picking up your line, there are two primary ways to handle signing them up:

Divide and Decide. This is where you collect information on the rep or the group and make a decision or representation offer after the show. This is more like a traditional interview-type process. You may want to check references and call stores in the rep's area to see how well they are received there. If you are lucky, you may need to take time to decide between two or more interested reps for the same territory.

Seal the Deal. Right there on the spot. If the rep or principal is really interested and you are too, why wait? If your gut says yes, then go for it. Make the oral agreement and shake hands. If you start to have second thoughts, you can go home after the show and research the rep. You can always change your mind before you sign a rep agreement.

No matter which way or combination of ways you go, just be sure to keep the rep informed about your process and where you are in it.

After the rush of the show, you may realize you are not as equipped to deal with reps as you thought. It is perfectly okay to call a rep and tell him or her you need more time before taking on an outside sales force. Trust us on this. You will earn points for your honesty. On the other hand, if you ask around and find out your new rep has a local reputation as a scumbag, it's okay to contact him or her and say you have decided to pursue other sales avenues.

A final word about sales reps at trade shows: Please do not pounce on anyone wearing a "Manufacturers Representative" badge who walks by your booth. Just because they are a rep does not mean they are the right rep for you, that they are available to pick up your line, or know anyone who is. Sales reps attending trade shows looking for new additions to their lines list will thoroughly comb the show and find the right lines for them. Do what you can in advance, but have some faith in the process too.

Handling International Accounts

You may be approached by accounts from outside the United States while exhibiting at trade shows, most commonly from Canada. It is important that you have an accurate understanding of how to handle order fulfillment with these accounts.

Generally, the cost of shipping is the most significant issue with international orders. For U.S.-based manufacturers, use the buyer's preferred shipping method. They will always know the least expensive way to get merchandise to them from the U.S.

Shipping internationally will involve custom forms and packaging that meets certain regulations. As of this writing, the international shipping fees are about three times those of shipping within the U.S.

Some international buyers may ask for a wholesale price discount. Generally, we do not recommend ever discounting your prices on products. You may offer to split the cost of shipping with an international account, if cost is a factor for them.

Schedule a Daily Wrap

One of the best things you can do for yourself, your productivity and your post-show clean up is to make time for a daily debriefing. When the show shuts down for the night, it is very tempting to close up your booth and run to the nearest bar. The last thing you want to do after a long day is administrative work, but taking a few minutes to wrap up unfinished business will save you hours later. If you have downtime during the day, you can process leads, catalog requests and even orders as you go; but chances are good you are going to be busy selling, networking, and wheeling and dealing, so you will need to get caught up later.

You can do this in the booth either before heading out for dinner or later in the evening back at your hotel. Or, if you are an early bird, block out time the following morning for your debriefing. Just make sure it happens before you report for duty the next day. So what should this daily wrap include?

First, recap the day. Who did you meet that you want to stay in touch with? Take some time to organize your orders. Add up your daily sales total to see how rich you are or to get a little kick in the pants about selling more the next day. Do as much as you can to start processing any orders you wrote. If you travel with a laptop, key all your leads into a follow-up template, calendar, spreadsheet or your customer database and schedule follow-up calls. Get any catalog requests loaded into a label template so they are ready to go. Answer and process any email that has come in and has not been handled. Check your office voicemail and make note of any calls that need to be returned. If you can, return those calls immediately; otherwise, make sure you either delegate or deal with them at some point during the next business day. Finally, gather up any receipts you might have and put them together in one place.

Do a daily wrap while the details are fresh in your mind. You will be doing yourself a huge favor by not letting these tasks pile up until you get home—when you will have to deal with them along with everything else from the show.

No matter what, *do not leave orders in your booth overnight*. Take them with you when you leave the exhibition hall. You do not want those orders getting lost or thrown away by a cleaning crew—and you need to protect people's credit card information.

Think ahead and get organized for the next day too. Did you run out of staples or did all your pens disappear? Did you eat all of your mints and need to restock? Do you have a meeting scheduled that you need to prepare for? Does your shirt need to be ironed? Take some time to get everything together the night before so you can sleep well and arrive confidently on the floor the next day knowing you are prepared and ready to go.

<table>
<tr><td>CHAPTER
6</td><td># Talking to Buyers and
Finding Your Sales Mojo</td></tr>
</table>

If you have skipped all the previous chapters and are starting with this one, please stop now. Go back to Chapter 1 and start again. The information that follows can only be fully utilized if you have a foundation in place to understand buyer personalities. The ability to anticipate and respond to their actual needs, as opposed to your perception of those needs, is an important skill. You also need to have the right tools to identify and take advantage of opportunities. Rather than jumping with both feet into the middle, back up and begin at the beginning; otherwise, you will spend a whole lot of time circling back to make up for the important steps you've missed. Cool? Cool.

Types of Buyers

There are basically three types of buyers you will encounter at a wholesale trade show. Each of them will be looking for different types of merchandise. They will also be looking for different types of deals.

Independent Retail Buyers. As a young or first time exhibitor, this is the primary buyer you will be working with. These buyers come from stores with one to three locations and include museum stores and catalog buyers.

Small Chain Buyers. These buyers come from regionally based chain stores that may have up to several dozen locations. Small chains can be a great retail outlet but be aware that they often request price or volume discounts and have specific shipping requirements. They may expect return and/or exchange privileges. Some may require a service agreement, meaning someone from your company is expected to conduct inventories, place orders and take returns at each of their locations.

Large/Big Box/National and Discount Buyers. You know who these guys are. These are the national retailers. They are the big league. You may be thinking that all you need is to land one of these big boys and you will be set. In fact, you may have even designed your line with one of these national retailers in mind.

While very sexy on the surface, these accounts are no joke. These stores are in the business of making money, not helping you grow your business. They have very specific requirements that are, typically, non-negotiable. National retailers will also have fulfillment and return expectations that are very different from independents or small chains.

> An industry friend of ours thought he had hit it big time when he landed an order from a well-known national retailer. He soon discovered the terms of sale required by this retailer were very specific: a 47% wholesale price discount and 100% return privileges. While the retailer would house the manufacturer's merchandise in their warehouse, the purchase order specified certain days of the week—and even a time of day—when they would accept deliveries from their own shipping company to their stores. He was docked for errors with delivery times and order fulfillment, even though this retailer's headquarters handled all of those issues internally. He was charged regardless of who was at fault. The final straw occurred when he was fined $250 in non-compliance fees for a $200 order. He was about to pull the plug on the deal when he was notified by the retailer that they would not be reordering because they only carried minor lines like his for one or two buying cycles.
>
> You can only imagine all of the paperwork involved with this type of fulfillment situation. As a one-man operation, he was buried. He later learned that other manufacturers who sell to national retailers often employ people who just work on those accounts full time. In the meantime, he has made it a company policy not to sell to any store with more than three-dozen locations.

Your company may be perfectly positioned to accommodate the specific requests of the big box stores. But realistically, most new and young companies are not yet suited to make these types of accommodations. Of course it is loads of fun to dream about being buried alive with orders; in reality, the process of preparing orders of this size is incredibly time consuming and stressful—not to mention the fact that you have to actually have the inventory in stock. Think carefully about your ability to comply with rigid terms of sale before going forward with national accounts, should the opportunity present itself.

Trade Show Buyer Personalities

Every buyer is going to be different; some will be incredibly friendly and outgoing, while others will leave you wondering how they even make it out of bed every day. But within the kaleidoscope of people who claim the title of "Buyer," our experience on the floor has revealed two primary trade show buyer personalities and three sub-groups of these personalities. The two primary trade show buyer personalities are:

Passive/Lookers. This buyer likes to simply be left alone. They might not say anything to you, other than hello. They are not interested in your pitch or in small talk. They may look at your display and just ask for a catalog or just do a quick walk through your booth and leave without saying anything.

Active/Engaging. These are the interactive types. They will engage you, listen to your pitch and ask questions. With these buyers you can showcase best sellers, talk up displays, and probably bond over the fact you have the same breed of dog.

The first subgroup of both buyer personalities is the *Hyper-Focused* buyer. These buyers are looking for one type of product. You may have a passive buyer who scans your booth and then suddenly asks if you have anything with ukuleles. An active buyer may spend ten minutes talking with you only to then ask to see everything you have with purple on it.

It is almost impossible to anticipate or prepare for these seemingly random, niche markets. Part of the fun of exhibiting is getting to be creative in these situations. This is an excellent example of why having booth helpers who are familiar with your product is important. You do not want to miss out on a big order because your back-up person did not know about your collection of rainbow unicorn designs.

The second sub-group is the *Power Shopper*. This is the buyer who may only be at the show for one day and has a lot of ground to cover. They move quickly, make fast decisions and usually just pick up catalogs. They are fairly easy to spot because they have a huge bag of materials. They quickly walk into a booth, look around, ask for a catalog, toss you a business card and they're gone.

The last sub-group is the *Spender*. These buyers will walk the show making purchases as they go along. When they have used up their budget, they stop looking and leave.

Talking to Buyers

"When we're in the booth, we're the faces of the brand, so we just try to be fun and friendly. *—Joel Gryniewski, Old Tom Foolery*

Someone steps into your booth. They are looking at your product. They look interested—happy, even. They whisper something to their companion. They reach out and touch something in your booth and smile. What do you do?

First, take a deep breath. Do not pounce. Give your guests some room to breath. Obviously, you should greet a buyer when they step into the booth. But hang back and do not start selling as soon as someone touches your giveaway or steps on your carpet. You are intimately familiar with your line, but this prospective buyer is probably not. Take it easy and give them a chance to take in the line. Just be cool, even if your heart and stomach are doing flip-flops at the idea of writing an order. Desperation, no matter how acutely you may be feeling it, never makes the sale.

"Please avoid the 'desperate, single girl' face. One year, we were next to the most adorable exhibitor with the most adorable product. They were so worried about making a sale they got shaky and desperate and we watched buyer after buyer get really uncomfortable in their booth." *—Randi Picarelli, Hard Cards*

We generally recommend leaving buyers alone until they touch something. Then, make your move. Make sure to greet or acknowledge everyone who steps into your booth, even if you are with a customer. Just say, "Excuse me" to the person you are working with and say hello to the new buyer or nod to them and give a "just a minute" sign. Then, immediately get back to the person you were working with. Most buyers will be patient and accommodating if you are working alone; but you can see how, again, having help in your booth can make a big difference.

"We always try to greet people as they enter our booth and then let the cards do the talking. We're there to take orders and answer questions, but we try not to be too pushy. Sometimes we feel like maybe we could make more money if we were more "sales-y," but that's just not our style." —*Joel Gryniewski, Old Tom Foolery*

A friend of ours is a buyer for a well-known museum shop. She tells this amazing story about stopping at a booth and being greeted very enthusiastically by a man working there. The booth was full of people and she could not get in to see one of the products up close. The man staffing the booth loudly yelled at her repeatedly from the back to "get back here and see this". He then proceeded to hound her and her buying partner, hovering close to them, talking constantly, and repeatedly interrupting as they attempted to discuss which products they were going to order. Finally, he just wore them out and they walked away.

Later that day, in another booth, she was not greeted at all and had to ask to write an order. She then watched in amazement as the person working the booth nonchalantly and apathetically went searching for an order form and a pen.

There is a sweet spot between overwhelming pushiness and underwhelming poor service: figure out where that spot is for you. It may take a couple of tries to settle in and get comfortable with it.

Avoiding the Show Badge Bobble

There is this trade show phenomenon we call the "Show Badge Bobble." The Show Badge Bobble is when an exhibitor's head bobs up and down rapidly as they look from a badge to a face and back again repeatedly. Sometimes it is much more subtle, and only the eyes flicker back and forth from badge to face and back again. It is quite a sight to see and tragically common on the show floor. We offer specifics about how to talk to buyers in the next section, but please be aware of this compulsion and do your best to avoid it. If you want to know someone's name or you are curious about where they are from, why not just ask?

It is tempting—and somewhat instinctive—to stare at people's badges and not look at their faces as they stroll past your booth, too; please try to avoid this. Make every effort to look people in the eye and greet them equally.

It is not unusual for buyers from well-known stores to turn their badges around to avoid being "recognized" by exhibitors. It is also not unheard of for some buyers to wear a badge that identifies them as being from another company so they can walk the show and browse in peace. The sad fact is that the senior buyer from Barnes & Noble gets a lot more attention and a lot more catering to than the owner/buyer from Paper Palace Card Shop.

We mention this only to point out that you never know to whom you are talking. Make sure to treat every potential customer with respect and give them the same level of service and attention, no matter how small—or big—their store.

You Had Me at Hello

Okay, you have "hello" down. But what happens after that? What do you say?

First, again, relax.

We recommend avoiding unproductive questions like "May I help you?" or "Are you having a good show?" You may have pairs of buyers who come into your booth and only seem interested in talking to one another. The easiest way to interact with them is just to say, "Please let me know if you need any help." Be careful to avoid slinking back into the corner of your booth; don't take their seeming lack of interest in talking to you personally. This can also be a good way to interact with a Passive Buyer personality because it establishes that you have noticed them and that you respect the fact that they just want to look in peace.

"[Selling] is not my strong area, so I know I make mistakes. I hang back and if someone comes in, I ask how they're doing. They usually ask how much something is and then we start talking. We don't have a pitch or a hard sell." —*Amy Smyth, Amy Smyth Made It*

"A trade show is a wonderful place to test attention-grabbers. What gets people to stop? To laugh? To say 'OK, fair enough, tell me more?' Test all show long. After the 100th pitch, you'll know exactly what gets people's attention. The show is also a fantastic opportunity for direct market research on your potential customers! Come up with three to five questions that you're going to ask people who walk by the booth, then ask away." —*Joyce Wan, Wanart*

Make an effort to engage in conversation with everyone. This may be uncomfortable for the more shy or introverted among us. Plus, people can be abrasive and sometimes downright nasty. We have said it before and we will say it again: do not take this personally. A sour mood on the part of someone else is totally about them; it's not about you or your line. Maybe they did not bring comfortable shoes or stayed up too late watching TV or missed lunch. Whatever it is, it is on them. Your job is to be happy, helpful and friendly, even to the Eeyores and Crabapples.

If you tend to be shy or soft-spoken, practice what you are going to say in the weeks leading up to the show. Run your greetings past people you know, or even by yourself in the mirror. Just like any performer, getting familiar with your script will make your time on stage easier to navigate. If you have a pocket full of things to say, you won't be at a loss for words—even if making the first move is not comfortable. If you are starting to wonder if you are reading a book on dating, you are not too far off. Many of the same rules apply!

"Work on improving your sales skills and go in with confidence." —*Megan Auman, megan auman*

When talking to people, start by looking them in the eye. Make every effort to avoid staring at their badge before or while talking to them. Start with a simple greeting, "hello," and introduce yourself. We like this so much more than, "What kind of store do you have" or "Can I tell you about the line?" We like it because the natural response from most people is to answer with their name. Voila. Connection! And, as in love, the #1 rule of selling is: be friends first.

Once you have the person's name, be sure to use it. You can then start in with other questions. Where are you from? What is your store called? What type of store do you have? Get this and other information directly from the buyer, not by looking at their badge and doing the Show Badge Bobble. Make the conversation authentic.

Let's look at an example:

> *Buyer walks into a booth.*
> **Card Company (CC):** Hi there.
> **Savvy Buyer (SB):** Hi.
> **CC:** Can I tell you about the line?
> **SB:** Thanks. I'm just looking.

And we have a dead end. There is almost no way to salvage this interaction without interrupting the buyer or passively waiting for the buyer to ask for help.

Let's try again:

> *Buyer walks into a booth.*
> **Card Company (CC):** Hi there.
> **Savvy Buyer (SB):** Hi.
> **CC:** How are you?
> **SB:** Fine. These kitten pictures are cute.
> **CC:** Thanks. The cards are all made in the U.S. and feature real fur from real pets and are printed with soy-based inks on 100% recycled paper and...
> **SB:** Hmm, that wouldn't really work for me. I have a shop in an allergy care center.

And our Card Company is left scrambling to recover. There is a good chance our Card Company is starting to get a little frustrated.

Let's see what happens the third time:

> *Buyer walks into a booth.*
> **Card Company (CC):** Hi there.
> **Savvy Buyer (SB):** Hi.
> *CC waits for the buyer to touch a card.*
> **CC:** Oh, you touched it; now I have to talk to you. That's the rule: you touch it, we talk. I'm Janet. Good to meet you. *Shakes buyer's hand.*
> **SB:** Hi, I'm Debbie. Nice to meet you.
> **CC:** Where are you from?
> **SB:** Baltimore, Maryland
> **CC:** Oh wow. My cousin lives in Baltimore. By any chance is your store on West 36th Street?
> **SB:** Yeah! Right on the Avenue.
> **CC:** Cool! He loves it there. Tell me about your store.
> **SB:** It's a cosmetics store in the front with a hair salon in the back and we sell a ton of cards.
> **CC:** Well, you're in luck; I have cards to sell. Do you niche your cards or have a general offering?
> **SB:** We have a general offering but our customers really seem to love hamsters and cupcakes.
> **CC:** Today is your double lucky day because I have both. Have a seat and let me show you the line.

Do you see what happened? The personal engagement helped the professional conversation flow more easily.

Obviously, not every conversation is going to go this smoothly, and these are pretty simple examples. The outcome remains the same: by looking for points of entry beyond the product and minimum order, the conversation can be furthered by opened-ended questions, a better understanding of what the buyer is looking for and an increased shot at the sale.

"Our cards generally break the ice for us. But we've lived in lots of different places, so we like to take note of where the customer's badge says they're from and mention something about that"
— *Joel Gryniewski, Old Tom Foolery*

Some people will connect with you, others will not. It does not matter. What matters is that you attempt to engage on a personal level first, business second. People like to do business with friends, or at least with people they are comfortable with.

Let's say you engage with a particular buyer, and you talk for a few minutes about how you are from Chicago and the buyer loves Chicago. You can easily slide into a product pitch by saying, "Well, if you love Chicago, you're going to love this Chicago-made line!" Make it faux-smarmy and fun. At the very least you will get a laugh. Then, hit them with the features of your line as well as your unique selling position (USP). If you are not clear about your USP, refer back to Part 1.

Once you've made the connection, keep it going. Soon, you will find yourself in a conversation with the buyer, and the product becomes the glue that holds it all together.

We also suggest not leading with the cost. That's right: do not start with the price. Point out the minimum quantities, the 100%-guaranteed sale for the first 60 days, the pigment-rich inks that are used to print the images, the fact that your product is U.S.A.–made, whatever your thing is. Let the customer bring up price. For some stores, even in this economy, cost is not a factor in picking up new lines. Do not make money an issue if it doesn't have to be.

Another option is to simply put your prices on the wall next to your product or on the product itself. Doing this avoids the discussion entirely and can help weed out buyers who are just focused on a particular price point.

Ask for the Sale

The hardest part for many companies is asking for the sale. That sounds a lot scarier than it is. Asking for the sale is, quite simply, saying "Would you like to place an order today?" If the mere thought of this leaves you queasy, you are not alone. Asking for money can be hard, especially if you are the creator of the line. Asking someone if they like your product enough to order it is the ultimate in exposure and vulnerability. We get it, believe us. We've both been there, repeatedly.

> "I just say, 'Would you like to place an order' and then they say 'Yes' and order. If they say 'No' or whatever, I say, 'Here's your catalog. Thanks a lot'." —Amy Smyth

Rather than looking at the money moment with anxiety and dread, approach it with the mindset of additional accommodation for your guest, or in this case, the buyer. This will work in either a "Yes" or a "No" scenario.

When the buyer says "Yes", invite them to sit down at the table in your booth. You will win big points by anticipating the buyer fatigue factor. Figure out ways to overcome it—an extra chair, water, or snacks. Make your booth a refuge for a weary buyer. Once they sit down, give them a chance to get settled while you get your supplies together. By the same token, some buyers will not want to sit down, so be prepared to grab a clipboard, an order form and a pen to take the order.

Many buyers will want help putting an order together, especially if this is their first order with your company. Have your best sellers already pulled out and bundled together and lead with those. Simply say, "Let me start you with the top sellers." Then, put the rest of the deck on the table for them to also look through. Remember your buyer personalities: your Passive Buyers will want to flip the deck uninterrupted—this means stop talking; an Active Buyer will maintain a conversation while looking.

"If they like [our line], they are going to buy it. If they have to pass it by someone, nothing we say is going to change that."
—*Stacey Rifkin, Hard Cards*

Sometimes, all your wit and charm are spent on the wrong person. You can spend a lot of time talking to buyers who are not the final decision makers. If you sense a conversation is not going to go anywhere, it is okay to simply offer a catalog and move on.

"We usually just wait for people to say they'd like to place an order. Or, if we think they're really likely to place an order, we might say something witty like 'Would you like to place an order'."
—*Joel Gryniewski, Old Tom Foolery*

Depending on your product, you may have rack or display programs available. Have a pre-pack of designs already put together. That way if a buyer says, "I want a spinner" you can say "Great. Would you like to pick the designs or would you like a pre-assortment?" Then, have that pre-assortment ready for them to look through. Your Power Shopper may ask for the pre-assortment, hand you a credit card and be gone in less than five minutes, saying good-bye as she stuffs the order copy into her bag and walks away.

When you write the order, take extra care to make sure your writing is legible. There is nothing worse than getting home at the end of a show with illegible orders. The buyer certainly is not going to remember, and will probably be irritated enough that they cannot decipher the handwriting either. Slow down and write clearly.

Be sure to collect complete and accurate shipping information. If the billing address is different, be sure to get that as well. Double check the phone number to make sure you write it down correctly. Some buyers will have stickers prepared to put directly on your order forms or a full credit sheet that will have all this information. Just be sure to staple it to the order form.

Depending upon the nature of your business, you can make the ordering really fun. This is a great way to start building your community of retailers and promoting them, as well as your company in the process. Since most convention centers are Wi-Fi wired, ask anyone who orders with you if you can take their picture for your "Friends Gallery" on your Facebook Business Page. Friend or Like them and link to their store while they're still right there in the booth. How cool will it be when you have post after post after post of all the new stores who are now carrying your cards?

Payment

As we reviewed in Part 1, it is customary to require first orders to be prepaid with a credit card. There will be some accounts that will ask for terms on their opening order. We recommend having first orders prepaid from everyone, even if the ship date is in the future. You can certainly take credit sheets and offer to set them up on terms for future orders. It has come to our attention that some of the larger manufacturers have done away with terms all together and require payment—whether credit card or check—at the time an order ships.

Keep the process simple and get your money faster by requiring prepayment on your opening orders. Be sure to double check that you have written the card number down correctly, including the expiration date and security code. If your processor requires a billing zip code, get that too. Ideally, your order form is designed in such a way that it has a space for all this information, and serves double-duty as a reminder to you to collect it.

Most buyers will want a copy of their orders for their records. Some will want that order totaled. Be prepared to do both. The easiest way is to have your order forms printed with a two-part NCR (non-carbon paper). This gives you one for the customer and one for you to take home for processing. You may be more high tech and have the ability to scan all your orders or even enter orders directly into a laptop in your booth. If you do this, make sure you regularly back up those orders and have a separate thumb drive for back up as well.

FAQs

So, what are the most Frequently Asked Questions you can expect to hear from buyers in your booth?

- What's your minimum order?
- Do you offer exchanges?
- What's your show special?
- Do you have a catalog?
- Which credit cards do you take?
- Can I order online?
- Where are your products manufactured?
- Where do you ship from?
- Do you give exclusives?
- Do you retail online?

As you can see, the kinds of questions buyers will ask are pretty straightforward. Having answers to these questions will be an important factor in establishing yourself as a company that knows what it's doing. Think about it. If an exhibitor cannot answer these basic questions, how is a retailer supposed to trust that the exhibitor will be able to deal with any real issues that arise? If you are a new company, many of these questions will be easy for you to answer if you have done proper pre-show planning.

Some buyers will ask more advanced questions like:

- Do you have a rep in my area?
- I don't work with reps, so how do I order direct?
- Who else in my town carries these?

You can see how having done the pre-show information gathering and organization we discussed in Part 1 will come in very handy.

"A certain amount [of exhibiting] is just trial and error. You can only be as prepared as you can be and the rest you just make up as you go." —Amy Smyth

---

"I always try to remind myself throughout the process that I am there to have a good time and to have a positive experience" —Barbara Wade, Indigo Paper Goods

---

What happens next is all part of the trade show magic. There are no guarantees of success, failure, or anything in between. There comes a point when your booth has been set up, you are ready to go and you just leap. You might make mistakes, but so what? You rework, reinvent and ride it out. Just do the best you can and by all means, try to have fun in the process.

For many exhibitors, the end of the show is the end of the road. Their trade show participation stops as soon as the crate leaves their booth. You may be tempted to do that, too. But do not forget about all that post-show planning you did in the initial stages of this process. What you do next can make all the difference in how the show pays off for your company.

In the next part, we will walk you through your post-show strategy and re-entry into your post-show life.

PART THREE

After the Show

7 Your Big Finish

You have just given an award winning performance on your trade show stage. The roar of the crowd is still echoing in your ears. The curtain has come down and the house lights have come back up. The audience has gone home and the sets, props, and costumes have all been packed away. You managed to not only survive the multi-day test of endurance, but you have also earned a standing ovation. Bravo! Bravo!

Now what?

What Happens To Your Booth

After the show closes, you will break down your booth and pack everything back up into your crates, return rented items and possibly give away some of the things you purchased onsite.

Many trade shows, in conjunction with the official freight company of the show, will warehouse your booth for you. If you have a cumbersome pre-made or custom booth, large display fixtures or furniture pieces, it may be more economical to pay to have your booth put into storage rather than pay to have the booth shipped back home. However, this only saves you money if you know that you will be returning to the show next year. Another option is to have your booth shipped to the next trade show you will be participating in and stored in that show's warehouse. Check with show management or the exhibitor guide for more details on what options are available.

If you do ship your booth to your home or office, make sure to store it in a cool, dry place. Create a checklist of everything you took with you as well as those items you needed to buy onsite to make packing for next time easier. And if you borrowed the stapler from your desk to take with you to the show, now would be the time to put it back.

No matter what direction your booth goes, be sure to remove any perishable items. Those candy giveaways will not last until next year. Not that we have ever made that mistake.

What to Do When You Get Home

"How important is follow-up? If you want to have a business, I'd say pretty freakin' important!" —*Amy Smyth, Amy Smyth Made It*

You will probably be ready for a vacation and seriously hoping to not have to think about this whole trade show business for a while. You have earned a break. But even though the show is over, your work is not. It's time for your curtain call: the Follow-Up.

One of the most important trade show success insights we can give you is this: what happens after the show is just as important, if not more, than what happens at the show. For many exhibitors, post-show plans involve little more than catching up on their sleep and enjoying not having to stand on their feet all day—both are admirable, legitimate and necessary goals. But there are countless opportunities missed and thousands of dollars in orders lost because exhibitors fail to keep the trade show momentum going by following up with leads, prospects and industry contacts after a show. Many of the companies we interviewed for this book reported that they often do more business in the six weeks after a show than they do on the floor. In case you were wondering why we put such an emphasis on the importance of creating a post-show plan in Part 1, this is your answer.

You cannot wait around and sit on those leads until you feel like following up. "What's the hurry? Why does timing matter?" you might ask. There is a magical thing that happens at shows that can be really difficult to jumpstart on your own: it is called momentum. Buyers are ready and their budgets are open to buy; their heads are full of ideas and they want merchandise for their stores, so it is important to take action now. Do not let those sizzling-hot leads go stone cold. If you ignore your show leads, you are just flushing money down the toilet. Be willing to do what some other companies are not. Your business and your bank account will thank you.

We know you are going to be tired when you get home, and that is where the real power of a well-organized post-show action plan comes in. If you have already created, scheduled and planned out the steps for following up, all you need to do is execute those steps... after you take a day or two off.

Where Do You Start?

Despite that fact that we are urging you to take action on your leads right away, make taking care of yourself your first priority once you get back home. Even if you get back in the middle of the week, take at least one day off to sleep and rest. Do your laundry. Let your dog—and possibly your spouse or partner—get reacquainted with you. Spend time with your family. If you can afford it, get a massage or a pedicure when you get home (you too, guys!). Take at least one day to just be easy with yourself. Drink lots of water, and again, make a conscious effort to eat healthy. If you exercise, be sure to fit in a workout, even if it is lighter than your normal routine.

You may also experience a little bit of the post-show blues. After all, you have just spent the past two or more months working diligently to get ready to exhibit. Now it is all over. Just like with any big event, it is not unusual to have an emotional drop when the event wraps. This is another reason why taking at least one day off and taking it easy for a few days is important.

Getting some extra rest post-show is physically important as well. Did you ever get sick in college right after your week of finals finished? That's because your body was running on less sleep and lots of junk food and caffeine, and sometimes pure adrenaline. The same thing can happen after a trade show. Even though you made your best effort to take care of yourself, your immune system may be vulnerable once the rush of the show is over. You do not want to be away from work for a week because you fall ill, so take care of yourself and stay healthy.

The First 48 Hours

You may be one of those super-slick types who is so adept at working remotely that you can stay on top of your game every minute that you are on the road. Email gets answered, orders get processed, receipts get turned in and coded and you still get eight hours of sleep a night. If you are that kind of super star, feel free to skip these steps. It will not hurt our feelings. Our guess, however, is that most of us—even the more tech savvy among us—still need to dedicate some good old-fashioned administrative time to our post-show strategy.

After being gone for a week or more, it can be very easy to spin into a spiral of multi-tasking and leave tasks half done as you pop off to the next one. Slow down! Everything will get done. Just be sure to work carefully and methodically so nothing falls through the cracks.

Here are the primary administrative areas to tend to on your first two days back in the office:

Snail Mail. Start by completely processing your snail mail. Do not just open it, look at it, and set it aside. Instead, open it, look at it, and make a decision about it. Then, in classic organizing style, pitch it, deal with it or delegate it.

Email. Next, clear out your email. If you travel with a laptop or can do email on your phone, this may not be a big deal. Fire up that email program and switch to working *offline*. Why offline? It eliminates disruptions—especially the constant new mail notification "bing"—that can be a huge time-eater when you are trying to process a lot of email quickly. By working offline, your concentration will not be interrupted by any incoming mail until you have cleared out the old messages. Just focus and bang it out.

Phone Messages. Depending on your office setup, you may have a landline in addition to your cell phone, and there may be additional voicemail to respond to. Ideally, you have been keeping up with these calls while you were at the show, but not everything can be handled remotely. If you changed your outgoing message before leaving for the trade show, most of your callers will be expecting to hear from you around now.

Allow a little extra time for these post-show return calls. You may find the retailers and reps who did not go to the show now wanting a full report of how it went. Do not forget to change your outgoing message now that you are back from the show. We have all called someone and heard the "I'm out of the office until June 3rd" message... and it is July 15th. Keep your professional image in place by making sure your outgoing voicemail message is current.

Money. At some point, you are going to have to deal with the expenditure aspect of your time at a trade show. Take some time to process your receipts; getting them together should be a snap if you collected them in one place while you were away. If this did not happen, collect them together now. You may need to dig down into the very bottom of your bag to find all of them, but do it. Your accountant or tax professional will be able to advise you on the specifics of which receipts you need to keep, as well as which expenses are tax deductable. For our purposes, we are going to focus on just getting your money matters together while the details are still relatively fresh in your mind.

If you manage your own accounts in a program like QuickBooks, go through those show expenses and get them entered into your system. If you work with an accountant or have administrative support, follow whatever procedures they have for the submission of receipts. Move this pile of papers off your desk now; do not put them aside with the intention, no matter how good, of dealing with them later. You will not remember any special circumstances or details if you wait too long.

Process Your Show Information. If you have not already done so during your daily debriefings, start by entering every business card into you database or Customer Relationship Management software program. Some of these people will be prospective customers that want a catalog or some type of follow-up; others will be existing customers who want new catalogs or would like to have a rep follow up with them; some may even be sales reps who want to talk to you about picking up your line. Then there could be some creepy guy you met at an industry function and you just want to flag him as a Do Not Pursue. Whoever they are, load them in.

Just as when you collected these cards in the first place, do not rely on your memory to recall details about the people you have met. Write everything down in their contact file. Since you made notes on the back of all those business cards as you went along, this is a simple matter of keying in data. Double-check to make sure you enter in all the information correctly. Your address book is useless if it is loaded with incorrectly typed phone numbers.

Give Thanks and Praise. Keep those contacts warm by sending thank you notes. Trade shows are a great place to start new relationships as well as build on existing ones. Many of the people you meet on the floor are going to deserve a thank you note, or at the very least a "great meeting you" note. This is the one part of your post-show strategy where you have the opportunity to really set yourself apart with minimal effort.

Remember, trade shows are about being friendly. There's no app for friendly; it is something uniquely personal. Thank you notes and "nice to meet you" notes are a simple way to make a great impression. Even the most curmudgeonly cranksters out there enjoy—or at the very least notice—the sophistication of a handwritten note. We can almost guarantee that your competition is only sending some lame "nice to meet you" email, if that much.

Thanking and praising is about making the effort to acknowledge someone else, not just doing what is convenient for you. Plus, if you are anywhere near the greeting card and gift industries, giving thanks and praise with a post-show handwritten note is doubly important. Seriously—smoke what you're selling.

Unless otherwise requested, we really recommend that you do not email your thanks and praise. In fact, we even have trouble getting behind those websites that will write, address and send the cards for you. They sort of defeat the point of the personal touch. The only possible exception to this would be if you work for one of those online card companies—then, you're cool. You have a get out jail free card. Nobody will judge you for promoting your own product. Not even us.

So, who are some of the people to whom you might send thanks and praise? We recommend starting with the stores who wrote an order with you at the show. If you wrote 20 orders or less, send a thank you note to every store that ordered. If you wrote more than that, sort out the top 20 orders and send notes to those customers. You do not need to limit yourself to the top 20, but there are other business issues to attend to besides writing thank you notes! Do not feel guilty about not writing to everyone.

You will also want to send thanks and praise to other industry people you met at the show. This can include reps, manufacturers, buyers, members of the press, show management and, if you really hit it off, your show neighbors.

Do not stress out about this; just be friendly and appreciative. And here's another successful insider secret: you can use the same formula—Greeting, Appreciation, Takeaway, Closing—for each note.

Let's look at an example of a thank you note using this formula.

The Greeting is just that: Dear Rob and Meryl.

The Appreciation is what you enjoyed: Thank you for the fantastic dinner at Burger King last week during the show.

Your Takeaway: I really enjoyed sharing our love of poodles, as well as talking to you about all the great new things coming up this year for Furry Pet Greetings.

And Close it up: I am really looking forward to working with you to help FPG grow. Thanks again, Janet.

This is, of course, just one way to write a thank you note. If you want more ideas, check out any of the hundreds of books available on business and personal correspondence at your local, independently owned bookstore. Or, if any of your customers are bookstores, ask one of them for a recommendation. Then—you guessed it—send them a thank you note!

Just a final word on this topic: if you are a greeting card company, it goes without saying that you should be using your own product for these thank you notes. It may seem ridiculous for us to even mention it, and it is not our intention to insult you; suffice it to say, without naming any names, we have good reason to make this point.

Get Involved Online. Make use of social media to keep the show momentum going, too. Friend, follow or link to the people and stores you met and start to include them in your virtual circle of contacts. Please note that if your company does not have a business page or feed and you only use social media to talk about what you are eating, what's happening on *The Vampire Diaries*, or your Farmville status, do not link with professional contacts until you are posting something that would be valuable to them. Personal connection is important, and you may develop friendships with many of these people over time, but keep it more professional in the initial stages. Besides, the point of connecting with these particular people is primarily to promote your business. The cute pictures of your dog come in a distant second.

Many of these tasks may already be completed or, at the very least, started during your daily debriefing at the show. If you are caught up on all of these things, great! If not, do not despair. You can easily use the initial days back from a show to catch up, get ready to take action on events and meetings, and further your sales mojo. Getting a head start while still at the show makes this even easier.

Dealing with Disappointment. If you left the show with minimal orders, an anemic amount of leads and a full candy bowl, you are probably feeling more than a little deflated and possibly questioning if you even want to continue with this venture. Finding yourself in this post-show scenario does not mean that you are a failure, that your product stinks or that the closest thing to cards or gifts you should get is working at the post office or as an elf in Santaland at the mall. A poor showing does not mean that your business is finished and that you should just throw in the towel. There is little doubt you learned a great deal from exhibiting, even if most of it is what not to do. Try to use those lessons to propel your line and your company forward.

A poor showing can also indicate several things about where your company is—or isn't. Before you choose the agony of defeat, give serious consideration to the following factors. Please note that some of the answers many not be easy to accept.

- Was your line really ready to exhibit?

- Did you have enough designs available?

- Were you in front of the wrong types of buyers?

- Was it difficult for customers to identify what you were selling due to inadequate or insufficient display?

- Do you need to reevaluate your product line?

- Should you consider enlisting the help of outside, objective resources?

- Are you selling a product for which there is no demand?

- Do your pricing and, consequently, your production costs need to be evaluated?

- How did your line stand up to the other companies you saw at the show?

- Was the artwork or text strong enough?

- Was the packaging appealing or practical?

- Did buyers looking at your display seem perplexed and confused?

- Was your booth chaotic and crowded and not showcasing your line adequately?

Ouch! These are tough, almost soul-searching questions, especially coming after months of preparation and the expense of exhibiting. However, they are important inquiries to make if you plan on continuing to market and promote your line or exhibit at a trade show again.

"I made my grand debut at the National Stationery Show with only 36 designs. I believe I made only $200 in sales—barely enough to pay for even lunch but I felt like it was such a valuable learning experience. I applied everything I learned at my first show to the following year's show where I ended up making at least 25 times the amount of sales." —*Joyce Wan, Wanart*

"I didn't sell crap my first year, but it's always a choice in how you react to things and how you determine the path you are taking. The way I see it, it's a choice of whether I am going to be miserable and cry in my soup, or whether I am going to keep a positive attitude and look at all the great stuff that happened."
—*Barbara Wade, Indigo Paper Goods*

As you can see, your first 48 hours back in the office are a nifty little combination of administrivia, laying the initial foundation of industry relationship-building and assessing the viability of your business. After four or more days of talking to people, being upbeat and flashing that star-powered smile, you may find the quiet days at your desk a welcome change from the bustle of the show floor. Enjoy them for the change of pace they offer and the fantastic opportunities for reflection and regrouping.

Within 14 Days

After you complete the first 48 hours of digging out and debriefing, it is time to get the ball rolling on catalog mailings, order fulfillment and securing sales representation. Generally, these tasks should be completed within two weeks of your return home from the show. It is also time to do a full evaluation of your show participation.

Process Your Orders. Quick turnaround is expected by your customers who placed orders with immediate ship dates at a show. If you took any orders that require you to call the buyer for a credit card, fill those orders first. Stores will occasionally over-order at trade shows. If you are the last one to call to get payment, you run the risk of hearing, "Sorry, we ordered too much at the show. Please cancel this order." This does not mean you should call the store from the shuttle on your way to the airport, but we do not recommend waiting more than two weeks. The early bird truly does get the worm, or in this case, the payment.

Please do not ship orders until you have successfully processed the credit card. Once the merchandise is in the hands of the buyer, it is nearly impossible to get a valid credit card number if the first one has been declined. It is better for an order to be delayed—and paid for—than shipped and in collections.

If you have orders with future ship dates, do not ship them or charge the credit card earlier than requested unless the buyer contacts you and asks for an earlier delivery. Buyers schedule shipments at specific times for inventory control and cash-flow purposes. Shipping before a requested date will only make your customers mad. You may find they refuse your package altogether and drop you as a vendor. Just mark your calendar now to remind you to ship the order.

> After my second time exhibiting at the National Stationery Show, I made a special effort to make sure I filled all of my show orders within one week. There was one order in the stack with a requested ship date of August 1st. I went ahead and packed the order, along with the others. I put it in the corner where I could see it from my desk.
>
> Slowly, from late May until early August, more and more paperwork, samples, deliveries and whatnot got stacked up on top of the box. In mid-September, I got a call from the store asking where their order was. I felt terrible and was horribly embarrassed. Needless to say, I did not tell them it was buried on the floor of my office.
>
> *– Identity hidden to protect the guilty*

If, for whatever reason, you anticipate problems filling an order as requested, contact the buyer. One of the top complaints we hear from retailers is lack of communication from manufacturers when items are back-ordered, sold out or delayed. Even if your answer is, "The glitter-covered, bejeweled shot glasses are not coming because the entire factory staff is now in rehab," make sure to communicate with your accounts. They are counting on that merchandise, and if fulfillment is compromised, you have a responsibility to tell them.

If you are working with sales reps, be sure to send copies of all show orders to them. This is especially important for any new accounts you may have opened at the show. Even if you do not pay them commission on the show orders, reps need to know what is going on in their territory and who placed orders at the show. If you grant exclusives, be sure to ask your reps if any new accounts in their territory are in conflict with existing stores before filling any show orders.

Disseminate Information. Chances are good that you have a stack of catalog or sample requests from existing and prospective customers. Since you have already entered all your new information into your CRM, sending these items out should be easy. Just pull the data, merge it into a label template and you are good to go. If the account placed an order at the show, you may want to include your thank you note with the catalog. It is not a good idea to put thank you notes inside a shipment, however. Deliveries are often unpacked by store employees, or even in an offsite warehouse, and personal notes can be misplaced or thrown away.

To Rep or Not to Rep. If you are considering new reps you met at the show, or have already signed them, get them up and running as soon as possible. If you have not committed to a particular rep, do your research and make decisions about representation. It is important to get rep kits in the hands of your new sales force as soon as possible. Hopefully, you will have some leads from the show to hand them as well. Many reps will schedule appointments right after the show with buyers who did not attend. Remember, your reps are going out on appointments whether they have your information or not. Get them the samples and supplies they need to show your line as soon as possible.

Just as with show orders, quick turn-around time is especially important for the show leads you are sending to reps; they should be sent within two weeks of the show closing. Since you have already compiled your CRM data, this should be easy to do. If you have not entered all the new information yet, you can literally tape business cards to a sheet of paper and fax them out. You will be a total hero if you also include a note with details such as what part of your line the lead was particularly interested in or if they took a catalog.

If you do not have show leads for a particular territory, contact the rep anyway. Use this as a chance to check in about how things are going for them.

Give them a show report if they did not attend. If they were at the show, ask how it went for them. If you spent time together at the show and you enjoyed it, tell them that too.

Day 15 and Beyond

If you have even one lead but have holes in your sales rep coverage, lead follow-up falls on you. No problem, right? But what does "following up" really mean, and how do you avoid falling into the follow-up abyss with every other show vendor?

The technical definition of "following up," according to Dictionary.com, is "to increase the effectiveness of [an action or thing,] by further action or repetition." It also defines it as "to pursue closely and tenaciously," which we especially love. More practically, though, following up is the action taken to get in touch with a buyer you have already made contact with—in this case, at a trade show. By doing so, you remind the buyer about your company and products, and take steps to further the relationship leading to a sale. As we have mentioned before, not all buyers are able or willing to place orders on the show floor. This is where the follow-up comes into play.

Starting about two weeks after the show, begin a direct round of follow-ups. Contacting a buyer earlier than this will most likely result in requests to call back after they have had a chance to catch up from being at the show. If you wait more than two weeks, those leads start getting as frosty as a cold call, and just about as effective.

Even with a prompt, perfectly timed follow-up, you may find yourself introducing your company all over again. Do not take it personally. Remember, buyers look at hundreds of booths, and they get just as worn out as exhibitors. This is where your notes written on the business cards you entered into your CRM come into play again.

Historically, trade show follow-up has consisted of the old-school dialing for dollars scenario; you sit with your list by the phone and dial one contact after another. The conversations usually go something like this:

"Hi, I'm Janet from Furry Pet Greetings and you stopped by our booth at the show."

Are you are groaning in agony? You should be!

Think about that phone call from the buyer's perspective. How do you think they would respond? Did you come up with something like, "Well, no kidding! I went to a lot of booths."

We've got $100 in cash that guarantees this type of call will generate this reply, "Okay, which company are you again?" To which you will stumble and stammer and say something along the lines of, "Oh, we have cards and gifts with pictures of furry animals on the front"—and you will get crickets on the other end. Finally, the buyer might give you a tepid "Oh yeah, okay," but you both know that the buyer doesn't remember your line. You both awkwardly play along anyway, and you end up sending a catalog with the promise to follow up again in two weeks. Hey, we have all done it!

Instead of banging your head against the desk, try getting creative with your follow-up. By investing a little bit of time in research before you pick up the phone, you might be able to warm up the call or get the information you need to write the order. Here is where social media and other free online tools can make all the difference.

Look up your leads and customers via Facebook, Twitter, and LinkedIn; add a Google search to the mix and really see what you can learn about them. Assuming you are using social media as a business resource and not for purely personal purposes, Friend or Follow leads and customers if you have not done so already. Send them a message introducing yourself and include a link to your company. This gets you on their radar and, with information about you right in front of them, even the foggiest of memories can clear up.

This research gives you a great deal of information about who they are and what they do before you even pick up the phone. On the surface, this may seem creepy or even a little stalker-like, but what it does is help you identify which of your show leads actually have the potential to convert into active accounts. Why spend months chasing down Petunia's Pens when a simple internet search reveals Petunia sells animal pens, not high-end fountain pens.

Another way to warm up your lead follow-up is to send a special email. Now, we know we just said not to send your thank you notes via email but this is not a thank you note. It is not just "Thanks for visiting our booth" on a fancy layout. Using a creative sales email as part of the follow-up process can be very effective in reminding a buyer about your line. There are so many free and easy-to-use services available, such as MailChimp.com, which let you send sharp-looking newsletter-style emails. You can use this as your initial contact and include a picture of you and/or your booth to help remind the buyer of who you are.

If you have a video camera, make a special "reminder" video: take some shots of you in the booth at the show; highlight some of the products in your booth as well. You can easily embed it in the email or add it as a link. Just make sure to keep it under two minutes. No matter how well done, no one wants to watch your eight-minute homemade commercial.

Many of these programs are set up so emails can be designed and even scheduled to mail in advance. By creating the basic layout as part of your pre-show planning, all you have to do once you return home is tweak the text and add in your show photos.

Although your email is just a little warm-up, why not ask for the sale, just like you did on the trade show floor? Offer a few more weeks to take advantage of your show special, or come up with something different. Whatever you decide, make it easy for any of these leads to take action. Include your phone number very clearly in the body of the email and include a live email link.

"Your follow-up email can't be spam-like. Personalize it and reference something you talked about. Be sure to include an easy link to your website or catalog PDF. Start with email first, if there's no response then call. Try twice before you give up"
—*Stacey Rifkin, Hard Cards*

Put an expiration date on any post-show promotion you offer through these emails. Not only does this create a sense of urgency for the buyer but it also gives you a reason to call any store that does not respond to the promotion. Then you get to say, "I noticed you didn't respond to my free freight promotion. I know you are busy trying to catch up after the show, so I thought I'd call and offer you one more chance if you order today." The expired promotion serves as a point of entry for a conversation with the buyer. A lack of response to the offer could mean that the buyer is simply not interested.

If you send this email to a store in any territory you have a rep in, be sure to tell the rep about the promotion and give them a chance to open the account. Do not circumvent your reps on this. If they have not written orders by the time the promotion has ended, check in with the rep to find out what happened with the leads.

When you make your round of phone calls, lead with something like: "Hi, this is Janet from Furry Pet Greetings. Is this a good time to talk?" Remember, buyers are busy, so respect their time. Assuming they say yes, continue: "I wanted to follow up on the extended show special I emailed you about on Tuesday. We met at the show and discussed our shared love of bratwurst and Oktoberfest." Use anything you can to jog the buyer's memory about you and your products. Ask them if they still have your catalog, if they have any questions, and if they are ready to place an order.

Of course, some buyers are going to shoot you down with no way to recover. One of our favorite rejection follow-up techniques is to ask if this is "no for now," or "no forever." If it is "no for now," ask when you should check back and then do it—on the exact day the buyer suggests, even if it is six months down the road. Remember, some buyers have atypical buying schedules or seasons; they may be looking today, but will not be placing orders for several weeks or months. This is often the case with brand new stores.

If the answer is "no forever," thank the buyer for their time and let them know you are there to help if they change their minds. Then send them a catalog and a hand-written note saying the same thing. If you are feeling really confident that your line is really right for a store that shot you down, give the buyer another call in about six weeks just to check in one more time. You can be funny about it, too and say something like, "You know I was thinking about you today and wondering if you had reconsidered the Furry Pets line? I'm not very good at taking rejection so I thought I would call you back to see if you really meant to say no." At the very least, you might get a good laugh. This is paper, not plasma. Have some fun.

Also keep in mind that selling is about solving people's problems. People buy stuff because they need it. They need to send someone a card because it is their birthday; they need to buy someone a gift because they are getting married; they need a thank you note for the gifts they receive. Selling is about being in place at the right time to be the solution for whatever someone needs.

When you sell your products to a store, you are solving the needs of their customers. Sometimes you may have to point out to a buyer that there is a customer need they are not filling, and therefore, a problem they are not solving. But for the most part, you are not arm-twisting a buyer into purchasing your products. What you are really doing is pointing out solutions to their problems. And if they can't see that you might be their perfect solution, then so be it.

With that being said, make sure you know what you are talking about. Listen carefully to the feedback your potential customers are giving you.

"I get calls from companies and sales reps all the time trying to sell me Washingtonian souvenirs. I always tell them the same thing: while we are located in Washington, DC, the majority of our customers are locals. They come into the gift shop to buy performance- and event-related products, not Washington, DC, souvenirs. You have to trust that buyers, ultimately, know what is best for their store."

—*Stephanie M. Fridge, Buyer, The Kennedy Center Gift Shops*

Don't Forget the Press!

Do not forget to include the industry press in your follow-up. If you did not meet any press members at the show, send a post-show follow-up press release to those you contacted before the show. They are going to need additional information for articles in future issues of their publications, so why shouldn't it come from you? You do not need to send them the same press kit again, though.

Following up with press is not as urgent as following up with buyers, and can certainly happen several weeks later than your direct sales calls. Be sure to check the editorial calendars of each magazine you submit to and send them information about your products that coordinates with theme of those upcoming issues.

Conduct a Post-Mortem

Do you remember those show goals we hounded you about setting in Part 1? Well, now is the time to get those goals out and use them to evaluate the success of your trade show endeavor.

Here are some questions to ask yourself:

- How many goals did I achieve?
- Were my goals realistic?
- What went well at the show?
- What did not go well?

- What could I improve or do differently?
- What should I do or not do next time?

Take some time and really reflect on your trade show experience from beginning to end. Some of your best moves may have happened at the very beginning. On the other hand, you may be able to identify things that happened later on that should definitely not be repeated. As you think this through, you may find it helpful to makes notes or even write out a full trade show recap. File this away with your other trade show materials and review it next time you decide to exhibit.

> "[My first time exhibiting] I got 13 orders and many leads, including a national account [that continues] to be my best customer. I picked up reps too. I didn't expect any sales so I was thrilled with what I got. It was fantastic." —*Amy Smyth, Amy Smyth Made It*

Depending upon how your evaluation and overall show experience went, you may be asking yourself whether the show was worth it or not. As we mentioned before, this is determined by a number of factors, many of which you may not be able to fully analyze until several weeks after the show. For now, do the best assessment you can, knowing that some of the gratification may be slightly delayed.

> "I think we walked away from [our first] show with 18 new accounts and lots of leads. Considering we printed 200 order forms before the show, our expectations may have been just a tad bit unrealistic! But, after sharing our experiences with owners of other card companies [in the weeks and months post-show], we realized we probably had a pretty decent first show."
> —*Lauren Gryniewski, Old Tom Foolery*

If you want to get technical, you can try measuring your Return on Investment (ROI), which is basically determining how much money your earned based on the amount of money you spent. The formula for determining your ROI is actually pretty easy, even though the term sounds pretty advanced. Here's how you do it:

Take the gross dollar-amount of sales you generated at the show and divide it by the cost of the show.

So if you took in $9,000 in orders and spent $3,000 doing the show, your formula would look like this:

$$\$9,000 \div \$3,000 = 3$$

ROI is expressed as a ratio. In this case, it would be 1:3, which means for every dollar invested in the show, you got back three.

Bear in mind, this formula is completely objective: it does not take into account the subjective benefits that are not quantifiable in dollar amounts, such as new reps, industry connections, and press contacts. It also does not take into account your manufacturing costs since every company's costs and profit margins will be different. You will want to factor those numbers into your overall assessment. But if you are looking at hard numbers, the ROI formula is the place to start. It will give you a rough idea of whether or not your show participation was profitable.

In its purest form, ROI does not take into account orders you receive as a result of follow-up. It only includes the orders you wrote at the show. You can include post-show orders in your ROI calculation in the weeks following the show, and we encourage you to do this. It will give you a much better representation of your ROI. We suggest putting a time limit on which orders get included. Generally, if an account you met at a trade show is going to order from you, it will happen within two months of the show's end.

There are many opinions about ways to follow-up and debrief after a show. What we have laid out here is a plan compiled from the best and most consistent steps and strategies utilized by the companies we interviewed, as well as from our own experience. Not everything will work for every exhibitor. It is much better to do something, even with limited results, than to walk away and leave money on the table without making any effort to get it. You have worked hard to get to this point so don't stop before reaching the real finish line. See the whole process of exhibiting through to the very end.

A Final Word

Making the decision to exhibit at a trade show is a big step in your company's development. Not only are you going to invest thousands of dollars in bringing your product to the world, but you are going to commit hundreds, if not thousands, of hours preparing for, working at and following up after the show as well. While the payoff of exhibiting at a trade show can be significant, the decision should be well thought out and your company needs to be ready.

Greeting card and gift companies alike dream of going to a trade show and hitting it big. They envision themselves returning with thousands of dollars in orders, a full roster of new sales reps, dozens of industry connections, and feeling like they rule the world. The good news is this can happen. The reality is it does not happen all by itself.

Showing up, looking sharp and writing orders are only part of the trade show success equation. As an exhibitor, you are going to spend several days talking to current and potential customers and selling your line. There will be opportunities to make important industry connections. You will also learn how to best describe what you do. By seeing how other exhibitors display their products, as well as your own trial and error, you will learn how to effectively display your line. You also will also have the benefit of being exposed to hundreds of other manufacturers, many of who are just like you. There is a tremendous opportunity to ask questions and share information with these other companies—not to mention the valuable feedback, both good and bad, you will receive from potential customers.

It is important to understand that the first time you exhibit at a trade show you might not write enough orders to cover your booth expenses. *This does not indicate failure!*

Many companies, especially new ones, need to make an appearance at a show several years in a row before buyers are ready to place orders and sales reps are ready to take them seriously enough to start showing their lines. Remember, trade shows are an investment.

This is not to say that there are not companies that enjoy tremendous success the first time out, but many of them have years of behind-the-scenes work prior to their trade show debuts. Getting your company and your products out into the world takes time, hard work, and strategic planning. It also requires consistent marketing and promotion, and trade shows are one of many steps in that process.

Although trade shows are an amazing place for your company to grow and to learn, exhibiting at one is not something that should be rushed into. There are many definitions of success at a trade show, but you should know that the most successful companies are the ones that walk in with a plan - and by plan, we are not referring to what logo-imprinted giveaways they will have or where they will go out for dinner after the show closes each day.

Successful companies have a clearly defined, measureable game plan that includes tasks, actions, contacts and research. This plan begins before the show opens, runs during the show dates, and extends long after the booth is packed up and the company staff returns home.

Successful exhibitors know what to bring, what types of people to talk to, how to behave on the show floor, how to ask for the sale and how to get free publicity. They know how to gather valuable leads and, more importantly, what to do with those leads after the show closes. You owe it to yourself and the success of your company to do as much advance work as possible before you even sign a contract or write a check to exhibit at a trade show.

You can also plan yourself to death. If you are waiting for everything to be perfect, you could end up waiting forever. Sometimes you just have to jump in with both feet: find a show that is right for your company, establish your budget, create your plan, and go for it. Only you will know when the time is right.

All the planning and pre-show work in the world will not compensate for an under-developed product line. Please make sure your line is really ready to show; otherwise, your dreams of stardom can backfire. If you have questions about what a sufficiently developed line looks like or other greeting card and gift business basics, we recommend you read our first book, *Pushing the Envelope: The Small Greeting Card Manufacturer's Guide to Working with Sales Reps* (Center Aisle Press, 2010). It is full of expert advice for getting your business together as well as proven strategies for finding, recruiting, and retaining sales reps. A line that is rep ready is generally trade show ready, and vice versa.

With consumer shopping making a huge migration to the Internet over the last decade, buyers are starting to follow suit. Many are starting to order wholesale without traveling to trade shows or even working with reps. There are some industry people questioning whether or not trade shows will even exist 10 years from now. We hope they do.

There is one big thing you get at a trade show that you just cannot get online: human connection. We are in a sentimental business and the ability to connect is critical—with customers, fellow exhibitors, sales reps, and press. Nearly six years ago, we met at a trade show and it changed our lives forever. It is unlikely our paths would have ever crossed otherwise. There is no doubt that amazing things can happen on the trade show floor; things that just would not happen anywhere else.

Just because you've reached the end of this book, does not mean you are on your own. This is only the beginning of the help and resources available to you. Visit our website: www.CenterAisleGroup.com. Send us an email, sign up for our newsletter, and stay connected to the industry. For more ideas, as well as all kinds of industry updates, you can also follow us on Facebook (Center Aisle Group) and Twitter (@CenterAisleGrp).

There is no real right or wrong when it comes to exhibiting, but there are benefits to learning from the experience of others. We hope this book helps you navigate your first—or your fifteenth—show with focus, direction and an eye on the goal of taking your business to the next level.

Here's to your success; we look forward to seeing you in the aisles!

Glossary

Drayage: The fee assessed for moving your show materials from the loading dock to your booth in a convention center or exhibition hall.

Emergen-C: A vitamin pack that dissolves in water. It will supplement your vitamins and help boost your immune system. Highly recommended before and during the show.

Exclusives: When a retailer agrees to carry a line and, in exchange, a manufacturer agrees to not sell that line to other retailers in a given area. Also called protecting territory.

Exhibitor Guide: The exhibitor guide is the handbook of all the rules and regulations specific to the venue and the show in which you will be exhibiting. It is generally published by the show presenter or management company and provided to you free of charge when you sign your show contract.

Freight: The cost of shipping your booth to the show's warehouse.

Installation and Dismantling: The set up and break down of a trade show. Also known as I&D.

Lead: Someone who contacts a manufacturer or rep directly and requests information about a product line.

Net 30: The invoice is due within 30 days of the invoice date.

Net 45: The invoice is due within 45 days of the invoice date.

Net 60: The invoice is due within 60 days of the invoice date.

Pipe and Drape: The metal framing and colored fabric used to create a wall, separation or curtain at an event.

Prize Pig: Trade show attendees who gobble up all the candy, catalogs, buttons and plastic tchotchkes they can stuff into a bag from any company that has them available.

Press Release: A document issued to the media that announces your company, your products, and related events.

Production Schedule: A comprehensive list of all the tasks that need to be completed and precisely when they will happen.

Sell sheet: A page, or pages, with high resolution, full color card images and greetings.

Show Badge Bobble: A trade show phenomenon that occurs when an exhibitor's head bobs up and down rapidly as they look from a badge to a face and back again repeatedly.

Show Directory: A book available to all show attendees. It contains a map of the show floor, a full show schedule and listings of all the exhibitors and their contact information.

Show Special: A promotion offered as an incentive to place an order at the trade show.

Takeaway: An information card or other item given out by exhibitors in place of a catalog.

Target Delivery Date: The earliest date and time your freight is allowed on the show floor, assigned to you by show management.

Unique Selling Position: Also known as your Unique Selling Proposition or USP. What sets your product apart from the competition and gives people a reason to buy. It defines a manufacturer's mission, purpose and identity.

Index

About the Authors

Rob Fortier is the owner and creative director of Paper Words. His card designs have earned him write-ups in industry magazines such as *GREETINGS etc, Gifts & Decorative Accessories, Art Buyer, Giftware News and Stationery Trends,* and have been featured on the HGTV cable network. He is the co-author of *Pushing the Envelope: The Small Greeting Card Manufacturer's Guide to Working with Sales Reps* (2010, Center Aisle Press). He lives in New York City.

Meryl Hooker is a Sales Rockstar helping individuals and sales agencies achieve rockstar results with a rockstar attitude. She is an internationally recognized speaker, consultant, writer and an award-winning manufacturer's representative. She is the writer of *Road Rage: The Blog* and co-author of *Pushing the Envelope: The Small Greeting Card Manufacturer's Guide to Working with Sales Reps* (2010, Center Aisle Press). She lives in Washington, DC and can be found all over the Internet.

Also available from

CENTER AISLE
P R E S S

Are your greeting card sales at a standstill? Do you want to move your sales beyond the local store to stores across the country? Have you thought about working with sales reps but have no idea where to begin? This is the book you've been waiting for. Finally, everything the small greeting card manufacturer needs to know about finding, recruiting and retaining a winning sales force can be found in this easy-to-read handbook. Written from both the manufacturer and sales rep perspectives, this nuts and bolts guide is full of industry information, sales tips and guidance for building successful and profitable rep relationships. Are you ready to push the envelope?

"Meryl & Rob's book offers a very clear, straight forward overview of starting and operating a savvy greeting card company and what it really takes to take the company to the next sales level..."
    —Vanessa Harnik, VP of Sales & Marketing. Notes & Queries

"What a wonderful tool for budding greeting card and gift companies. If we had access to this information when we were getting started, our lives would have been much easier. Everything you need to get started is right here." **—Cathy Henry, J-Dig Cards**

"An insightful, witty and comprehensive guide to the greeting card industry. This book contains everything you need to know to get started in the industry whether it be as a manufacturer or sales representative... Way to go Meryl and Rob!" **—Beth Safran, Principle, What's In Store**

Available at **www.CenterAislePress.com**

CPSIA information can be obtained
at www.ICGtesting.com
Printed in the USA
BVOW09s0210011217

501667BV00002B/204/P

9 780578 081588